Thirty Years in the Trenches Covering Crooks, Characters and Capers

By John Drummond

CHICAGO SPECTRUM PRESS
4848 Brownsboro Center
Louisville, Kentucky 40207
800-594-5190

ISBN 1-886094-00-0

Printed in the U.S.A.

10 9 8 7 6 5 4

For Carol, Beth Ann, Duncan, and Frank.
You put up with a lot of long hours and long days.

ACKNOWLEDGEMENTS

I would like especially to thank Arthur Caudy for his help. Arthur shot the cover photo for the book and had the tedious task of shooting pics of our various subjects off a television monitor.

Of tremendous value was WBBM-TV tape editor Gary Wright. Gary, on his own time, made still stores of our subjects from video tape. That enabled Caudy to proceed with his unenviable assignment.

Kudos must also go to Robert Sadler and Dick Drott of the Chicago Police Department's Crime Laboratory. They volunteered to pose for the cover shot after putting in a long day at the crime lab. And we cannot forget Roth Moi the "corpse" on the cover photo. Fortunately Roth survived that cold September evening without even catching a sniffle.

This book could not have been written if it were not for my many former colleagues at WBBM-TV. They included assignment editors, producers, and management types who would lend an ear when I made a pitch to do a certain story. And finally the mini cam crews and tape editors who shot and edited the stories that made it on the air and eventually ended up in this book. These are the folks who really toil in the trenches. Thanks also to WBBM-TV executives who authorized us to use Channel Two News video as illustrations in this book.

And last but not least our thanks to Dorothy Kavka of Evanston Publishing, Inc., who made a number of timely suggestions that made our task a bit easier.

TABLE OF CONTENTS

INTRODUCTION

I call it "feeding at the trough," the TV reporter no sooner arrives at his or her desk, then presto, the reporter is handed an assignment and is sent to the motor pool to rendezvous with a mini cam crew. The reporter has had no time to work the phones or attempt to enterprise a story. Pleas that the reporter needs time to develop a story that he or she has been working on are often ignored. "Get to the scene," the reporter is told, "we'll talk about that later."

More often than not, the above scenario is the daily fate of a TV general assignment reporter in a major or medium seized market. The reporter will wind up that day toiling with other grunts in television's version of trench warfare.

Author doing standup at Starved Rock State Park,
scene of 1960 triple murder.

The story, the general assignment reporter is being sent out on, is usually a mundane affair, a run of the mill yarn, it rarely will be the lead story. There will be nothing exclusive about it. The other broadcasting outlets or newspaper or newspapers will also be sending journeymen reporters to the same scene. But the story will help fill a broadcast, particularly on a lean newsday. Those kind of stories range the gamut from a routine shooting, an over-night fire, a zoning dispute to morning traffic tie-ups and minor power outages. In the jargon of the business those kind of stories are done "quick and dirty."

Sometimes the reporter can put a different spin on the piece or luck out and find an angle that his or her rivals have overlooked. But as a general rule the merchandise available and time restraints put the kibosh on any enterprising skills the reporter may possess.

"Trough feeders" have little time to wax eloquent. Most local TV operations are obsessed with story counts. That is, a certain number of stories must air on a specific newscast. A minute and a half seems to be a magic number to show producers. Sometimes a minute fifteen or a minute ten is the time cap that faces the G. A. Reporter as he prepares to record his narration. And when you include "sound bites" within that time frame, the reporter has little opportunity to write with any flair.

There are instances when the story the general assignment reporter is working on, turns out to be the biggest thing on the show's menu that day. A routine fire becomes a terrible tragedy, where a number of children have perished. A story about a stream that has over-flowed it's banks results in the flooding of a suburban sub-division. A hazardous material spill forces a large number of residents to be evacuated from their homes. Or a police officer or politician drops a bombshell during an interview.

That type of situation puts a different slant on things back in the newsroom. The powers that be then decide it's time to send their big guns into the fray. The G. A. Reporter gets big footed out of the picture. The station's anchorperson or star reporter arrives on the scene with carte blanche when it comes to time and resources. The unfortunate mike holder might still get a small piece of the pie, perhaps being sent to the hospital to talk to victims of the disaster or do interviews with neighbors. In the nomenclature of the business such interviews are known as ''MOS''(man on the street).

Sometimes, though, the reverse occurs. The anchorman or favored reporter is dispatched to what the assignment desk believes will have blockbuster potential. But after assessing the situation, the anchorman or his producer calls back to the desk indicating that the story is mediocre at best. The "dynamic duo" pulls up stakes and leaves. A lesser light is summoned and he or she ends up pinch hitting for the star. The story no longer gets top billing. But that's all in a days work for those who toil in television's trenches.

I remember one time in Chicago during the mid 1970s where a hostage taking incident turned out to be a major story. An anchorman was assigned, but after reaching the scene and realizing that a reporter from a rival station has scored an exclusive interview with the hostage taker, the anchorman, not wanting to play second fiddle, wisely opted to seek greener pastures.

A journeyman from the reporter pool was driven by courier to the site where he was steamrolled by the opposition who had garnered the exclusive interview. But that's life in the big city. After all, as they say in the military, "RHIP," rank has it's privileges.

Before we proceed any further, don't get the idea that you need to hold any benefit for a general assignment reporter. Although he or she may be on the low end of a news director's pecking order, the reporter, if working in a major market such as New York, Los Angeles, Chicago and other large cities is probably making a very good buck. In fact, more dough than his or her colleagues who are employed as general assignment reporters in the same city's newspaper or newspapers.

Although no heavy lifting is involved most general assignment reporters earn their money. They do not have bankers hours. Many a time I recall answering a phone call around two A.M. The call was not to tell me that my ship had come in and I had won the lottery. Instead the caller was somebody from the Channel Two assignment desk advising me to "Drop my.... And pull up my socks" and head to the scene of some fire or some other tragic development.

Being rousted at some ungodly hour does not mean that the G. A. Reporter will be done for the day after eight or nine hours on the clock. Often the grunt will be live from the scene for the six o'clock news and on a few occasions will still be at it during the prime time ten o'clock newscast.

The long hours were the rule during the late 1960s and early 70s when marches, demonstrations, and disturbances of one kind or another seemed to be the order of the day. Show producers and assignment editors were reluctant to pull out their soldiers from a potential trouble spot, even though nothing had happened and nothing of significance was likely to occur.

Often the assignment editor would inquire if rival stations were still on the scene. If they were, the reporter and crew would have little choice but to sit around and twiddle their thumbs until their rivals from the other channels vamoosed. Unfortunately the same scenario would be played out at the other stations. There management, playing the "CYA" (cover your ass) game, would keep their troops on the scene until the other crews decided to call it a day. The result was a stalemate that seemed to go on forever.

This was during an era before cable and VCRs had entered the picture. It was a time when newscasts attracted huge shares of the television audience. The networks were in their heyday and the OTO's (stations owned by the networks) such as WBBM-TV, WMAQ-TV, and WLS-TV in Chicago were coining money. Thus, overtime costs were not a problem.

In justice to news management protests and marches were the big stories of the day during the late 60s and early 70s. In Chicago there were riots after the assassination of Dr. Martin Luther King. That same year, 1968, were the Democratic Convention riots and a year later, the Days of Rage, where the Weather Underground went on the rampage. At the same time were countless disturbances at Chicago public high schools. And then there was the saga of a group of Native Americans who took over a Nike site on Chicago's lakefront and kept authorities at bay for days.

I remember working the street at that time. It seemed like some kind of revolution or civil war was about to erupt. There were protests of one kind or another every day. And television played a role in making it appear that the situation was even more serious than it actually was.

Many of the reporters, producers, and assignment desk personnel were of the same age and had the same socio-economic background as the protesters. They were sympathetic to the views of the anti war groups and would go overboard to accommodate their requests for television coverage.

One Saturday I was assigned to cover an anti war demonstration at what was then called the civic center in downtown Chicago. We found a total of eight placard carrying demonstrators marching around the plaza chanting anti war slogans. It was hardly any indication of grass roots support for their cause. Yet video from that minuscule demonstration made the air that night, purporting to show how the masses were up in arms.

On another occasion I was in the newsroom when an assignment editor took a call from a protest group. The caller wanted to know when a camera crew would be available to cover their demonstration. The caller said the TV station could name the time and place and the protesters would show up with banners and bullhorns. Believe it or not, the assignment editor was all too willing to accommodate the demonstrators until a couple of people in the newsroom objected.

Anti war groups weren't the only ones to get into the act. I was assigned to a different kind of demonstration one Sunday morning. A group of northwest Indiana residents was concerned over a certain railroad crossing that they considered very dangerous. They called the newsroom stating that they would be demonstrating at the site on Sunday morning.

Upon arrival we found a group of people sitting on the grass or in cars reading the Sunday papers. Once they spotted us, the group went into action and began marching around the RR crossing. After we shot tape of the protesters and interviewed a spokesperson for the group, we departed.

But after driving five blocks we stopped our truck and waited for about ten minutes. Then we drove back to the RR crossing. I wanted to see if the demonstration was still going on. I suspected it was not. I was right, the protesters were nowhere in sight. The demonstration was strictly geared for TV coverage. Once the camera crew left, the demonstration was over too.

The protesters had a legitimate complaint. The railroad crossing was dangerous. But the protest by the citizens was staged for television. Those Hoosiers from northwest Indiana and other citizen groups were finding out, like the anti war crowd, that television coverage could be theirs for the asking

But that was then and this is now. In these days TV news management takes a more realistic view of protests that have become so common place they are often ignored. Only demonstrations with large numbers of participants get any ink and with few exceptions, that is the way it should be.

Although demonstrations are no longer in vogue, TV producers seem to have a fetish about turning minor snowfalls into Armageddon. Weather is a major staple of local news. No question about it some viewers watch the ten o'clock news just to catch the weather forecast. Most major TV stations have trained meteorologists on their staffs to forecast the weather. They certainly provide a necessary supplement to a balanced newscast, particularly when threatening conditions exist.

But I've noticed in recent years that stations in Chicago and other markets have gone hog wild with teases or headlines blowing minor snowfalls and thunderstorms out of proportion.

If you live in the upper midwest you have to expect a certain amount of snow each winter. Yet two inch snowfalls are often treated by local TV as potential killer blizzards. It's a great way of attracting viewers. Doomsday predictions of a major storm are sure fire audience grabbers.

One time I was being sent out to cover one of the seasons first snowfalls. The station had already been promoting our coverage, hinting that a paralyzing snow storm might be in the works. I protested noting that the Weather Bureau and our own weather people were predicting two inches or less of the white stuff. I said there was nothing to indicate that any kind of heavy snow was on the way. The producer grinned at me and said: "don't worry about it, we're going to make it look that way."

The viewing public is not as gullible as some TV types apparently believe. I've heard more complaints about blowing storms out of proportion than any other kind of story that gets heavy hype.

I once got off an "El" train following a day at work when a well dressed stranger approached me saying, "Drummond, how can you live with all that crap you had on the air today about some big storm? You guys knew that there was nothing like that in the works."

I could hardly offer any kind of rebuttal. The stranger was right.

Another facet of TV news that I find annoying is the practice of sending reporters all over the globe when their is no local angle.

A case in point was an earthquake in Los Angeles some years back. This was not the quake that devastated L.A. In the early 90s but a tremor that caused only limited damage. At any rate a Channel Two reporter was flown to Southern California and was told to expect to do a live shot upon arriving at Los Angeles International Airport.

The reporter, through no fault of her own, had no idea of how much damage had occurred or if there had been any loss of life. When she got to the airport she called WBBM-TV where a writer read her some wire service copy about the quake. That was just about all the information she had about the incident. She went outside the airport and via a live satellite feed told her Chicago audience what was going on in L.A. The same information could have been given from our newsroom in Chicago. But management thought it was the greatest thing since sliced bread.

Viewers have often asked me why local reporters are sent to foreign countries when network correspondents, seasoned in the customs and mores of the nation, are already there. They file stories that are available to affiliates and stations owned and operated by the networks. Unless there is some local angle it's pretty difficult to convince these viewers of the wisdom of such a pilgrimage.

There are cases when stories are so big that dispatching your own people to the scene makes sense. The 1991 Gulf War was an example of that. The war had so many ramifications that even if there weren't any Chicago GIs in the combat zone it warranted expanded coverage.

So too did the 1995 Oklahoma City bombing. Those stories are the exception rather than the rule. Sending your own people to plant the flag in Timbuktu or other points unknown may be good for the reporter's ego.

But there are other ways for a news director to allocate his resources, particularly in these belt tightening times, when station managers are crying poor mouth.

Hyping snow storms or foreign odysseys weren't issues when I broke into the business. TV news was in it's infancy during the 1950s with many stations allotting only fifteen minutes or thirty minutes at most for their prime time newscasts.

As a general rule, the anchorman or newscaster as he was known then was most often an announcer and not a broadcast journalist. You will note that I used the term anchorman and not anchorperson. Female newscasters were a no-no in the 1950s.

Although I had some experience in radio as a high school student in the late 1940s, I didn't have a full time job in broadcasting until 1958. Four years in the air force and six years in college as an undergraduate and a graduate student were sandwiched in between.

Radio stations were beginning to realize in the late 1950s that there was "gold in them there hills." Having a local news operation was not only profitable but it kept the FCC off your back.

When I landed my first full time job, I started at the top. I became news director at KBIZ in Ottumwa, Iowa, a full timer as they call it in the trade. In show business terminology, places like Ottumwa were called tank towns. The pay was lousy, the hours long, and most of the news stories we covered were boring. To fill our many newscasts we not only reported on the doings of the Ottumwa City Council, the Wapello County Board of Supervisors, and the police blotter, but we also provided our listeners with the latest in births and obituaries. The "Irish sports pages" or "Irish scratch sheets," as the newspaper death notices are called by some people, are a staple of small town radio newscasts.

For a person entering broadcast news, a stint in a small or medium market station is an excellent way to learn the trade. So too is a job in a place like the City News Bureau in Chicago where rookie scribes face a sink or swim situation.

In cities like Waterloo, Iowa, Rockford, Illinois and Des Moines where I worked after leaving Ottumwa, there were no producers or interns to assist a reporter. *The Wall Street Journal, USA Today, the New York Times* and the *Washington Post,* where network personnel often get their story ideas from, won't help a fledgling reporter assigned to cover the Blackhawk County Board of Supervisors or the Des Moines City Council.

In smaller markets reporters learn to cover beats, to make contacts, and enterprise stories with little or no support help. If I was in news management I'd be reluctant to put any reporter on my payroll who hadn't served his or her apprenticeship in a small market or with an organization like the City News Bureau.

In many ways broadcasting reminds me of organized baseball. At one time the sport had a plethora of minor leagues that were designed to enable youngsters to show their wares and hone their skills. With the exception of a few Mel Otts or Bob Fellers, ball players had to work their way up to the biggies the hard way, by toiling for a few years in the minor leagues.

Some people in the television industry have a tendency to look down on those who opted to remain in small or medium sized markets. There are talented people in those outlets who prefer the lifestyle in smaller communities. It doesn't necessarily mean that they are less talented than their colleagues who try to find the pot of gold that major markets or network positions offer.

When I came to WBBM-TV in the summer of 1969, after a two year hitch as a newsman at WIND in Chicago, I did more than my share of "feeding from the trough," but there were times when management unleashed me from such a role and I was able to work the phones, meet with contacts, and come up with stories of my own. This work, for the most part, deals with stories we enterprised when we weren't running with the rest of the herd. This book, however, is not about the biggest stories that occurred in the Chicago area in the last thirty year or so. You won't read about the Daley years, the convention riots, the Helen Brach mystery, the life and times of Tony Accardo, the Plainfield tornado, major airplane crashes and headline stories of that mold. Not that we weren't involved in the reporting of those kind of stories, but so much has already been written about them, that we'll take a raincheck and leave them perhaps for another day.

Although most of the yarns contained here occurred in Chicago the setting could be almost any large urban area. Some of the people we focused on were headliners, most were not. Some were well known, others were not. One was a war hero, another a sport legend. Some could be described as real characters, others would fall into the category of villains. But all had one thing in common, they at least in my opinion were newsworthy.

Other authors have had more colorful and exciting backgrounds than yours truly. Our time has been spent toiling in TV's trenches. But in those trenches we met a lot of fascinating people. They had fascinating stories to tell. Here are some of them…

CHAPTER ONE

Smile for the Birdie

If you are in the news business you don't need an IQ of one hundred and forty to know that stories about the Mob sell newspapers and boost TV ratings.

In Chicago the local chapter of the crime syndicate is known as the Outfit and is never called by locals as the Mafia or La Cosa Nostra. Some Chicagoans follow the fortunes of their favorite Outfit figures as closely as they check out the standings of the Cubs or White Sox.

We once did a story for our ten o'clock news called "Bashful Bad Guys." Basically the piece showed how some Outfit members would go to great lengths to avoid being photographed. That's the kind of stuff TV producers love! You offer them a story that shows a Mobster trying to slug a photog, or somebody trying to leave a courthouse with a newspaper over his face, or a defendant running down the street like a track star, well, most producers are in hog heaven.

Now, if I was a Mob honcho I would issue a code of conduct to my minions. It would go something like this: "When leaving the courthouse tell the reporters, 'My lawyer has told me not to discuss the case. But I will say that these are scurrilous charges and I will be vindicated by a jury of my peers.'"

Hey, this guy sounds and acts like John Q. Citizen and not Public Enemy Number One. Not good television and not very interesting reading either. Not the kind of stuff that makes the front page or the ten o'clock news.

Tony Accardo — Chicago Mob boss, appears at U.S. Senate hearing. He never spent a night in jail, Accardo would boast.

Outfit soldiers should look to the late Tony Accardo as an example when it comes to courthouse decorum. Accardo, arguably the most powerful Mob boss of all time, wouldn't talk to news people when he came in or went out of various Federal buildings. But "J.B." or "Joe Batters" as Accardo was called by close associates never attempted to batter media members or try to hide from them either. He would briskly walk by a pack of newshounds, saying nothing but "no comment." On a rare occasion he would utter a "good morning" or "good afternoon." Accardo didn't look or act like a hoodlum in public.

Accardo's top lieutenant, the late "Joey the Doves" Aiuppa took a different tack. Aiuppa, at least in his younger days would take umbrage when he was spotted by scribes. The nickname "Doves" had nothing to do with Aiuppa's views on the Vietnam War. Instead the moniker stemmed from a Kansas hunting expedition Aiuppa made in the early 1960s. Aiuppa and some cronies were arrested after they bagged some nine hundred doves. The shotgun carnage outraged conservationists. That's when some enterprising newspaper guy pinned the name "Doves" on Aiuppa.

When we first started covering Aiuppa in the 1960s Joe would put a handkerchief over his face when photographers were present. That was Aiuppa's standard operating procedure for a long time. Then one day in the early 1980s we spotted him heading for a grand jury appearance at the criminal courts building. The sight of a TV crew and a still photographer set Aiuppa off. Joe tried to kick the still photographer and after charging the TV crew, he had words with the cameraman challenging him to a fight.

Joey "The Doves" Aiuppa was in a foul mood when he spotted a Channel Two News crew waiting outside the Criminal Courts Building.

The pictures of the "Doves" turning into a hawk made interesting television to say the least. And the incident rankled Aiuppa for a long time. Years later I was riding in an elevator with Aiuppa at a Kansas City courthouse where he and some associates were on trial. Aiuppa said to me: "You know I don't mind having my picture taken. But I don't like it when someone jams a camera right next to my face."

Aiuppa did have a valid point. In this case the cameraman was too aggressive. He was so determined to get "good tape" of Aiuppa that he almost climbed on top of the "Doves." Had he gotten any closer the two men could have rubbed each others noses. I told Joe it wouldn't happen again. That seemed to mollify Aiuppa. Later Aiuppa had a knee operation which reduced his mobility. He had to use a walker but his condition improved enough so that he was able to move about with a cane. Joe soon began making a number of trips to courthouses and camera crews would swarm around Aiuppa like sharks at feeding time. There was little that he could do about it but grin and bear it. Frankly, I think Aiuppa in his later years actually enjoyed all the attention he was getting from the media.

Big Joe Arnold was another guy who would get hot under the collar at the sight of a camera. According to investigators, Arnold at one time looked after the Mob's vice operations in the Rush Street area.

Big Joe, a husky six-footer who scaled well over two hundred pounds, had his share of run ins with the law. On one occasion Arnold was unhappy when one of our mini cam operators taped him in the lobby of the Dirksen Federal Building where he was making a court appearance. Photog Jim Ryan had just completed his task and had put his heavy mini cam on the floor when Arnold approached him and whispered in his ear.

"If you do that again, I'll knock your block off."

Big Joe Arnold got "hot under the collar" shortly after he was photographed in the lobby of the Dirksen Federal Building.

Big Joe's threat didn't set too well with Ryan and his mini cam buddies. So the next time Arnold showed up at the Federal court house there were two camera crews on hand. Arnold has slipped into the building unnoticed but after his hearing he was seen leaving the courthouse through the north entrance. Cameraman Bill Burk and Soundman James "Foots" Williams gave chase. They caught up with the burly Arnold on the sidewalk. "Big Joe" went ballistic. Putting his head down Arnold charged the crew ramming soundman Williams against a parking meter. But Arnold's El Toro act failed to discourage the crew. They stuck to Arnold like a fly on paper. And in the melee Arnold almost lost his pants and left the scene with a newspaper over his face.

Had Arnold simply ignored the TV crew and walked down the street his court appearance probably would have never made the air. Instead the station got plenty of mileage that night from the adventures of "Big Joe" Arnold.

William "Butch" Petrocellli, a feared enforcer and reputed hit man would also go to great lengths to avoid having his picture taken.

In 1977 Petrocelli was on trial at the Federal building on charges of firearms violations. "Butch" would boast to cronies outside the courtroom as to how he was able to evade a Channel Two news crew that was stationed in the lobby. One day we decided to put a full court press on Petrocelli by posting crews at both entrances of the courthouse. Then we could show our viewers what he looked like.

Petrocelli may have had a strong reason for being camera shy since he was a suspect in at least six gangland murders. Being seen on the tube might result in somebody fingering him. Petrocelli usually had a small entourage with him including an older brother who was a Chicago cop. Also in Butch's camp was a private investigator whom he had retained for the trial.

The cagey Petrocelli knew there were two camera crews waiting for him in the lobby. So he sent the private eye downstairs. The gumshoe began conversing with a couple of building guards. Before you could say "Jack Robinson" a guard had opened a side door that was supposed to have remained closed. Petrocelli darted out quickly. He had evaded us once again. We assumed that the private eye had paid the guards off but we couldn't prove it.

Several weeks later I ran into "Butch" at a boxing awards dinner at a suburban hotel. Petrocelli approached me and said:

"Was youse sore about what happened at the Federal building?"

We told Butch we weren't sore at him but at the guards who we suspected of being paid off by someone in the Petrocelli camp.

Bill got nervous though when he saw that I had a camera crew with me. In two instances that evening Petrocelli came up to me and stated that he didn't want his picture taken. We told "Butch" he could relax since we didn't want to embarrass our hosts by showing tape of a feared Mobster attending their function.

But "Butch" had thrown down the gauntlet and getting tape of Petrocelli became a priority at WBBM-TV. And we didn't have to wait very long. Two months after the boxing dinner we were tipped off that Petrocelli might show up at the wake of a small time gangster. Sure enough he did.

Not realizing he was on Candid Camera "Butch" was the cock of the walk as he strutted down the street, combing his hair, looking like a man about to go out on the town. It was vintage Petrocelli. The tape of Bill at the funeral home proved very valuable. It was the only moving video of Petrocelli in our library. And we got plenty of use out of it. You see, still pictures and graphics are fine but moving pictures of a subject are the name of the game.

It wasn't long before Petrocelli became a victim of gangland retribution. In December of 1980 Petrocelli vanished from his suburban Hillside home. You didn't have to be a Rhodes Scholar to figure out that "Butch" had probably been hit. About two months after Petrocelli disappeared police found the body of the feared Mob enforcer in the back seat of his car that had been parked on a west side street. His throat had been slit and his face had been burned beyond recognition. As of this writing the murder of Petrocelli remains unsolved.

Because Mob figures are often indicted, sometimes hit, or in the news for one reason or another major news organizations will usually allocate resources to obtain video of such subjects. The bottom line to the Outfit, the next time a camera crew tries to capture you're golden smile, relax and enjoy it. It's like painless dentistry, it will be over before you know it...

CHAPTER TWO

Speak No Evil

One veteran law enforcement official once told me, "you can't fight the Mob under the Marquis of Queensbury Rules."

Well, the Feds finally got a chance to use the legal equivalent of brass knuckles when the Safe Street Act of 1968 and the Omnibus Crime Control Act of 1970 were approved by Congress.

The legislation gave law enforcement new investigative tools to fight organized crime. One tool turned out to be a powerful sledge hammer in that fight. Title III of the '68 crime bill gave Federal agents wide latitude in the use of electronic surveillance.

Soon, Mob figures found out their phones were being tapped, their meeting places and cars had been bugged, and worst of all, some of their underworld colleagues were wearing concealed tape recorders.

Racketeers, who in the past seemed immune to prosecution, found themselves in the dock. The Justice Department began seeking indictments in cases, that earlier would have been considered unwinnable.

Defense attorneys found it very difficult to rebut evidence when jurors heard their clients whispering in conspiratorial tones to an informer on audio tape. There was even more damaging evidence when the defendant wasn't just heard talking about breaking the law but seen doing it on videotape.

One of the first high profile trials where government wiretaps put a nail in the defendants' coffin was a 1982 case in Chicago. A jury found Teamsters President Roy Williams, Chicago businessman Allen Dorfman, Mob figure Joey Lombardo, and two other men guilty of conspiring to bribe a former U.S. Senator in a land deal.

Author at left. At right, Teamsters President Roy Williams — convicted in Federal Court of trying to bribe a U.S. Senator.

The FBI had planted an electronic bug in Dorfman's office that became, as they used to say in vaudeville, the show stopper. Without those taped conversations, involving Dorfman and the others, it's very unlikely that prosecutors Doug Roller and Gary Shapiro would have ended up with a conviction. In fact, I doubt that the Feds would have even sought to indict the defendants without the tapes.

It wasn't long before the Outfit became paranoid about electronic surveillance. Speak no "evil" became the order of the day.

Soldiers were told to use pay phones when contacting their superiors. Scores, contracts, and Mob business were not discussed on the phone unless pre-arranged codes were used.

It was often taboo to discuss family business in public places for fear that a bug had been planted, possibly even at a favorite booth or table. So when the boys devoured big T-bones or porterhouses, the conversations were usually mundane.

Despite such precautions, loose lips continued to sink ships. Old timers brought up with the code of Omerta, kinship and honor, were dumfounded when it was revealed that long time con-

25

federates had become what the Mob considered "rats and stoolies."

Not only had some of these double crossing, long time denizens of the underworld been cooperating with the "G" but they were also wearing a wire. Often the Mobster would unknowingly spill the beans to the defector who he trusted like a member of his own family.

What the older Mobsters didn't understand was that times were changing. Younger hoodlums were more concerned about themselves than they were about the welfare of their own street crew or own crime family. They were looking after their own interests and were eager to strike a deal with the government to avoid prison.

In exchange for trading a black hat for a white one, the defector usually gets a light sentence or no sentence at all. Eventually he'll wind up in the Federal witness protection program and if he minds his "Ps and Qs," it's likely that he will be safe from gangland vengeance.

The result was that the Justice Department seemed to have an endless supply of Mob defectors who were willing to be wired for sound.

It wasn't long before crime syndicate members began falling like tenpins. Instead of wintering in Palm Springs, Florida, or Arizona, Mob honchos were trying to get sun tans at Leavenworth, Atlanta, or Lewisburg.

In the process of covering many criminal trials in Chicago, I've collected dozens and dozens of transcripts of taped conversations between defendants and informants. Some of those conversations turned out to be "smoking guns," others gave insight into the character of a defendant, and some turned out to be humorous. Others were rather boring.

The transcripts of tape conversations that we are going to be examining here, will give the reader a little of the flavor of certain criminal cases. We are submitting only small segments of these transcripts. Some of the conversations taped by Federal agents seemed to go on forever. Those marathon conversations could make a book in themselves.

ROCKY INFELISE

Ernest "Rocky" Infelise bears a striking facial resemblance to the late Mob boss Al Capone. Like the unlamented Capone, both men were in the rackets. Infelise never achieved the notoriety of Capone but "Rocky" was no slouch either. At one time Infelise headed a powerful Chicago street crew that controlled gambling, juice loans, and other rackets in parts of the city and the north and northwestern suburbs.

Unfortunately from Infelise's point of view he ran into a Federal juggernaut back in 1990. That's when he and nineteen of his underworld colleagues were indicted on a variety of criminal charges, ranging from gambling and racketeering to murder conspiracy.

Until the roof caved in on him, the burly Infelise was not aware that one of his key aides, William "B.J." Jahoda had been cooperating with the government. Not only had Jahoda been informing on Infelise and his minions, but "B.J." had worn a wire and even allowed the Feds to set up a concealed video camera in his Lake Shore Drive apartment.

At times Infelise seemed to pour out his soul to Jahoda whom he obviously trusted. Infelise said things that he would later regret. Some of the chats he had with Jahoda came back to haunt him. That was certainly the case in a September, 1989 conversation that was recorded for posterity. In one of the most explosive tapes ever played in Chicago Federal Court, Infelise was heard complaining about the over-head he faced each month in running a major gambling operation. A hushed courtroom heard Infelise boasting on tape that he had to take care of both jailed Mobsters and law enforcement officers. What follows is a portion of the transcript that became headline material:

Infelise: "I tell you, the fucking nut we got with these coppers, OK"

Jahoda: "Oh."

Infelise: "I lay out, I lay out thirty five thousand a month for guys that are away, and the coppers. That's not counting the workers, that's just the nut. You know it's getting rough."

Jahoda: "Jesus Christ."

Infelise: "Between you and I..."

Jahoda: "No, I mean, I knew you had the ten with the..."

Infelise: "...ten goes to the Sheriff."

Jahoda: "Yeah, with the Bohemian."

Infelise: "Yeah."

Jahoda: "But I had no idea."

Infelise: "Five goes, five goes to another guy."

Jahoda: "I got no right to ask this question, what the fuck do you get for ten thousand a month?"

Infelise: "Well, the Sheriff never bothers us, B.J. Then we got a guy in the States Attorney's Office. We've got another guy downtown..."

IRS agent Thomas Moriarty testified that Jahoda had identified former Cook County Undersheriff James Dvorak as the "Bohemian."

The reference to the "Bohemian" and alleged pay offs to the cops for protection was the talk of the town. Infelise's attorney, Pat Tuite scoffed at his client's tape recorded boasts. Tuite told reporters that Infelise, in effect, was trying to sound like a big shot by blowing a lot of hot air.

Dvorak who also served for a time as Cook County Republican Chairman denied he ever took money from the Mob to lay off it's gambling operations. Dvorak though, did have his share of legal problems. In 1993 he pleaded guilty to accepting bribes in connection with another case. But a Federal Judge ruled that the U.S. Attorney's Office never proved that Dvorak was paid off by Mobsters.

Some say Rocky Infelise looks like Mob boss Al Capone.

Infelise, a World War II army airborne veteran, probably had more of his conversations recorded by the government than any other Chicago Mob figure.

Those tapes revealed that "Rocky" would get hot under the collar when things weren't always going his way. One of those diatribes occurred in October of 1989 when Infelise vented his spleen in a phone conversation with his aide, Jahoda. "B.J." complained of feeling ill and told Infelice that he was unable to leave his Lake Shore Drive apartment to meet with him as had been planned earlier.

Jahoda's alleged illness did not set well with the "Rock." He ordered his subordinate to keep the appointment:

Jahoda: "R, I'm having dizzy spells. I just fuckin', I'm half fainting in the elevator. I can't even get out of this God damn building."

Infelise: "Walk down the mother fuckin' elevator. Now you called

29

me, made me come all the way from the South Side. I just pulled up over here. You get over here. I don't give a fuck how you get here. You understand? Don't be playing fuckin' games with me."

Jahoda: "I'm not playing games with you, Rock. How can you say that?"

Infelise: "Get over here. Right now. You hear what I'm saying?"

Jahoda: "I hear what you're saying. What do you want me to do, Rock? I can't even fuckin' get in a God damn elevator."

Infelise: "Walk down the mother fuckin' stairs then."

Jahoda: "Rock, maybe we better talk about this some other time. I'm up on the forty first fuckin' floor."

Infelise: "Listen, you cocksucker. You don't get over here, you forget about everything. You hear what I said?"

But Infelise didn't get in the last word after all. Jahoda's testimony and the tapes sealed Infelise's doom.

In August of 1993, a Judge threw the book at the "Rock." He was sentenced to sixty three years in prison. At the age of seventy one, Infelise's jail term amounted to a life sentence.

LOOSE LIPS SINK SHIPS

The fear of being overheard by "big brother" soon became an obsession with many members of the crime syndicate. But despite precautions some of the boys would still become blabber mouths as they talked over the phone or conferred with a confederate in an office, restaurant, or car.

Joey "The Clown" Lombardo was like a modern day Paul Revere. Lombardo constantly warned his associates, not about the coming of British redcoats, but about the onslaught of bugs and phone taps. Don't get fooled by the nickname of "The Clown." Joey is a pretty shrewd character.

Lombardo would often remind his colleagues that "loose lips sink ships" and Joey would admonish underlings not to talk business over the phone, in their homes or offices.

A good example of Lombardo's fear of being recorded came in a 1979 wiretap. Joey was upset because businessman Allen Dorfman had accepted a call from a crony who was under Federal scrutiny. Dorfman, an insurance executive, was controlled by the Mob and reported to Lombardo. Joey tells, Dorfman that the man should have contacted him from a pay phone. What follows here is an excerpt from a transcript of an FBI recording:

Lombardo: "Why didn't you have him call from a public phone?"

Dorfman: "Well, I'm going to arrange, find out what's a good time to call him from somewhere else."

Lombardo: "You call from a public phone."

Dorfman: "Huh?'

Lombardo: "You should call from a public phone."

31

Dorfman: "Yeah, that's what I'm going to do."

Lombardo: "Let me tell you something, you can hear it (garbled) me now. Wire tapping, illegal wire tapping, legal wire tapping, Anybody talking with these, bugs could be in your office, on your phone."

Dorfman: "I am very conscious of the fact, heh, heh, heh, very conscious of that."

Allen Dorfman — murdered by Mobsters who feared he'd "spill the beans."

Although Dorfman may have been aware that he was the target of a wiretap, he didn't act that way on the phone. And he apparently had no idea that the FBI had planted a bug in his Chicago office. That bug provided Federal authorities with a gold mine of information about illicit dealings involving Dorfman and his pals. Information that led to Dorfman's conviction as we pointed out earlier.

On another occasion, the Street smart Lombardo complained to Dorfman about, what he perceived, as constant surveillance on him by the "G."

Lombardo: "...it's brutal, it's brutal. In the office. Your number one on their fucking hit parade. I'm number one on the hit parade. Tony's (Spilotro) number one on the hit parade. And you absolutely die, Allen."

Dorfman: "When I was in Vegas. They assigned Metro (police) to me twenty-four hours a day. They told me. (They) came right out and told me."

Lombardo: "You are, you are, uh, you uh, you could say fuckin' big fuckin, man and they think you are the fuckin' man."

Dorfman: "Sure."

Lombardo: "Because you show wealth, you show this. Ya mean? Now me they know I'm something. They've got a pretty good fucking idea who I am and I got heat 'till I die. Fucking phones. You saw me talkin' on phones. I don't say nothin', and even when I do this, if the caller uses this number, this, this, this in your office. I don't say nothin' on that either."

Dorfman was considered a valuable asset to the Outfit with his ties to the Teamsters Central States Pension Fund. But that did not prevent him from being gunned down, gangland style, outside of a suburban hotel in early 1983. Mob superiors apparently felt that Dorfman might flip and reveal syndicate secrets in an effort to avoid a lengthy prison term.

Joey "The Clown" Lombardo shares a laugh with the author, and a court buff. Lombardo (in the middle) claimed he had nothing to do with organized crime.

Even the cagey Lombardo would, on rare occasions, talk out of school. One of those few instances occurred when Lombardo became angry with Morris Schenker, the operator of the Dunes Hotel in Las Vegas. Lombardo's friend Dorfman was upset with Schenker because Schenker apparently was dragging his feet on a debt. Dorfman had told Lombardo earlier that Schenker owed him a kickback from a Teamsters Union pension fund loan that he and former Teamsters President Jimmy Hoffa had set up.

A conversation involving Lombardo, Dorfman, and Schenker occurred in the office of Dorfman's Amalgamated Insurance Company where the FBI had planted a bug. Lombardo, after introducing himself, plays the "heavy" and goes to bat for Dorfman. He hints that Schenker won't live to celebrate his next birthday (73) unless he comes across with the moolah:

Lombardo: "The reason why I'm here, you don't know who I am. My name is Joey."

Schenker: "I assume you're all right because you're with Allen."

Lombardo: "Allen belongs to Chicago [the Chicago Mob] now, you know what I mean when he belongs to Chicago?" I just to have to bring a message back [from top Mobsters]. Let me tell you something. If they make a decision and they tell me to come back and bring you a message to pay, you can fight the system if you wanna, but, I'll tell you one thing. You say you're seventy two and you defy it. All you can do is send a guy like me to jail, one guy."

Schenker: "I'm not going to send anybody to jail."

Lombardo: "But, excuse me, but you ain't gonna send the system to jail. I'm just telling you, if they come back and tell me to give you a message and if you want to defy it, I assure you that you'll never reach seventy three."

I don't know if Schenker decided to play ball with Lombardo and Dorfman. I do know that he reached his seventy third birthday. Let's just assume that Schenker got the message and opted to cooperate.

As for Lombardo, Joey was convicted, along with Dorfman, Roy Williams and two others in what was known as the Pendorf case. Lombardo received a fifteen year sentence for conspiring to bribe a senator. Later another Judge added on ten more years after Lombardo had been found guilty in connection with a Mob scheme to skim money from Las Vegas casinos. Joey served the two hitches concurrently and was back on his home turf in 1992.

Although Mob watchers said Lombardo was a natural to take over the helm of the Outfit, Joey has contended that he has gone the straight and narrow route. In a 1993 interview with this reporter, Lombardo scoffed at allegations that he was either the head of the Chicago Mob or soon would be the top man.

Lombardo remains embittered over his 1982 conviction for conspiring to bribe a U.S. Senator. He told me," I went to jail for telling a guy to buy a piece of property."

PAY UP — OR ELSE

When FBI agents received court approval to tap the phones of a Southwest Side racetrack messenger service, the Bureau got quite an earful. What started out to be an investigation of gambling activities at the messenger service resulted in a nice bonus for the "Federales."

Incoming and outgoing calls involving James "Jimmy" Inendino, the proprietor of the messenger service, revealed the existence of a large scale juice loan operation.

Intrigued by what they heard the agents, along with some colleagues from the IRS, also put a tap on the phones at Inendino's house in Cicero. When they listened to some more juicy tidbits, the Justice Department decided to get the goods on "Jimmy."

In May of 1978, a contingent of law enforcement officers raided both Inendino's messenger service and his Cicero home. The raids netted some twenty three thousand dollars in cash. But of more significance, investigators seized a book containing the names of more than one hundred juice loan customers. Investigators said the customers owed three hundred thousand dollars on their loans.

Prosecutors who said Inendino supervised the juice loan operation, called it a three million dollar a year racket. According to the Justice Department, Inendino and his cohorts charged interest of two and a half to five percent a week. That amounted to one hundred and thirty to two hundred and sixty percent a year.

Loan sharkers don't care if the principal is paid as long as the debtor pays his weekly interest known as juice. Many of Inendino's customers were gamblers who had had a bad run at the track or at the tables. Others were small businessmen, unable to get loans through normal lending channels.

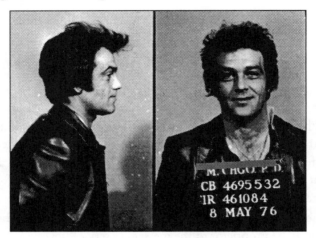

Feds got an earful when they bugged James Inendino's home and office. Police photo.

Inendino's clients were not forced to take out juice loans. They did so of their own volition because they weren't able to obtain cash anywhere else. But once these individuals got into debt, they were like flies, caught in the spider's web, unable to get out.

Inendino and his associates were not exactly diplomats when they suggested to recalcitrant debtors that it was time to pay up. Investigators said taped conversations between Inendino and his terrified customers provided a chilling insight as to how collectors threaten physical violence if debtors fail to meet their required payments.

Inendino never beat around the bush in dealing with his clients. He got to the point quickly, pay up or else. Government agents were listening in March of 1978 when Inendino read the riot act to a customer, identified as Chuck. Chuck is on bad paper because he is late in coming up with two hundred dollars that he owes. The following is a transcript from part of that phone conversation:

Inendino: "I'm not gonna call ya, I'm not gonna look for you. If it ain't here by six o'clock tomorrow night you write you own epitaph, you understand?"

Chuck: "I we, I'll tell ya I wanted to call ya yesterday but nobody answered the phone, nobody was home yesterday."

Inendino: "Don't tell me nobody was home yesterday, I was home all fucking day."

Inendino: "…If we don't see you tomorrow by six o'clock, you don't owe nobody nothing, is that clear Chuck?"

Chuck: "Yeah, well I Jimmy, I'm…"

Inendino: "You have it here by six o'clock tomorrow night or, uh, believe me when I tell ya, and I promise ya this, believe me I promise you, I'll break every fucking bone in your body before I got to jail, every fucking bone in your body. I swear to my kids, you understand?"

Chuck had company when it came to being chewed out and threatened. Others also had to face Inendino's wrath. One of those hapless individuals was identified in court documents as "Mike the Egyptian."

Mike apparently was a broken-down horse player who couldn't stay away from the racetrack. In this May, 1978 phone conversation Inendino accuses Mike of squandering money on the horses. Mike says no, but "Jimmy" doesn't buy it. Inendino wants Mike to fork over the eighty dollars that he owes.

Mike: "I don't have the money, if I got, I give you ya know, ya know that."

Inendino: "Your fuckin' ass."

Mike: "I swear to God, ah Jimmy, don't get mad."

Inendino: "Your fuckin' ass, you're a fuckin' liar."

Mike: "…I swear to god, I stay home, ask Bobby."

Inendino: "You stay home your ass. When you get paid, what do you do with your money, when you get paid? You go gamble at the racetrack. Am I right or wrong?"

Mike: "I, I swear to God. I don't go no place. I swear to God I don't go no place."

Inendino: "…talk to you cause I'm gonna hit you with the fuckin', I'm gonna hit you with a fuckin bat when I see you."

We don't know if "Jimmy" used a Louisville slugger on Mike. But it sounded as if Inendino had gotten his point across.

Frank Butera. His boss Jimmy Inendino said he looked like a bounty hunter.

Investigators said that Inendino would sometimes send one of his musclemen to call on a delinquent debtor. One of Inendino's enforcers was Frank Butera, a husky twenty-eight-year-old Chicagoan. In this March, 1978 tape recorded phone conversation Inendino psyches up his "tiger" who is about to visit a juice loan client. A government transcript from part of that chat between Inendino and Butera follows:

Inendino: "...Do you look all bearded up?"

Butera: "Yeah, I look like a fucking madman."

Inendino: "You look like you wanna eat chairs?'

Butera: 'Yeah, yeah. Okay?"

Inendino: "Ah, you gotta get that beard trimmed today."

Butera: "Yeah I know, I know, it's been botherin' you."

Inendino: "Yeah, it's you look grubby."

Butera: "Well."

Inendino: "You look like a bounty hunter."

Butera: "Jimmy, that's real nice, you talkin' to me like that. I look like a bounty hunter with this beard huh?"

Inendino: "Fanooz."

The wiretaps sounded the deathknell to the Inendino operation. Four members of the juice loan ring, including Inendino and Butera pleaded guilty to Federal racketeering charges. Inendino's guilty plea came after he had earlier been convicted of conspiracy to steal semitrailer trucks.

In September of 1978, Inendino was sentenced by Federal Judge Bernard Decker to twenty years in prison. Inendino was sentenced under a provision in Federal law that permits stiffer jail terms for defendants considered dangerous offenders.

Inendino served much of his time at the Federal correctional facility near Oxford, Wisconsin. Despite being incarcerated, Inendino was still raising "dough." He worked as a baker at the prison.

CHAPTER THREE

They Weren't the Real McCoy

THE BOMB SCARE

Not all television stories that are shot and edited make the air. Some get knocked out of the box because of a breaking news story such as a plane crash or a big fire. Others never reach the tube because of time restraints. A live guest or an anchor person gets long winded and the piece is shelved. The story then never sees the light of day because it is dated and is old hat for broadcast at a later date. Then there are other stories that are "killed" by management for a variety of reasons. The bomb scare yarn is an example of the latter. It never even made it to the editing room and with good reason.

One bright day in 1977 I was assigned to check out a story that sixty two missiles, containing hydrogen bombs, had been planted by Russian agents in Chicago area waterways. The bombs supposedly could be activated by remote control radio signals. The bulk of these missiles allegedly had been placed in the Cal Sag Canal and the sanitary and ship canal that are located just southwest of Chicago.

I assumed somebody was pulling my leg when I was told to see if any aspects of this wild tale could be true. Management told me that they too were skeptical of the missile report but they argued that it was better to be safe than sorry. They suggested that I start working the phones.

I called George Mandich who at that time was the spokesperson for the FBI office in Chicago. Mandich was well aware of the missiles story. And as absurd as the tale sounded, Mandich said, the Bureau had looked into it. So too, Mandich told me, had the Illinois Department of Law Enforcement and the U.S. Coast Guard. According to Mandich, the investigation by the three agencies had found the story of hydrogen bombs in Chicago area waterways totally unfounded. Mandich said as ridiculous as the allegations were, authorities had little choice but to make a search for the "bombs." If the government had failed to check it out, Mandich reasoned, there would have been cries that law enforcement was in league with the Soviets.

What triggered Channel Two's interest in the case was a call from a retired northwest suburban businessman, Edward "Sky" Powell. Powell felt that Federal and state officials had not thoroughly investigated the bomb threat. Powell, it turned out was a member of a group called the American Patriots Committee. The committee was then headed by a Washington attorney by the name of Peter Beter, a zealous anti-communist.

Beter had been sending a flock of audio tapes to his followers warning of the dire peril facing the U.S. It was Beter who apparently had marked on a map of the Chicago area where the hydrogen bombs had been planted by the Russians.

To make a long story short, the station insisted that I take a mini cam crew and interview Powell at his home near Barrington. I felt such a trip would be a waste of time. But we got our marching orders and away we went.

I found Powell a delightful host who was obviously well to do. But he was obsessed about the hydrogen bombs, feeling that Beter was on to something. We listened to one of Beter's tape recordings that told of the crisis facing the U.S. The August, 1977 report by Beter said in part:

"The Soviet program of planting nuclear weapons in the inland lakes and rivers of the U.S. has turned into an all out attack on our country. Soviet agents in vans, campers, and trucks were fanning out unhampered throughout our land, turning our peaceful countryside into an unsuspecting battlefield, strewn with nuclear bombs capable of destroying our water resources. And at no level of government, local, state, and Federal was anything being done about it."

Pretty chilling stuff, if it were true. Beter even contended that a Russian fleet was anchored off the east coast ready to launch guided missiles at major American cities.

Powell was concerned that authorities in Illinois weren't taking him seriously and that lawmen had not undertaken a thorough search for the devices. He explained that the nuclear devices were hard to detect because they contained what he said was a hydrogen peroxide propellant that buried each bomb at the bottom of the waterways. Powell complained of a conspiracy of silence by the government brass over the bomb threat.

We sat straight faced during the interview but it was hard to keep from cracking up. After all, some sixty nuclear devices planted by Russian agents right in our own backyard did seem a bit farfetched. If it was gospel I would have had the story of the decade. Powell, who we were told later, had been a successful engineer until he retired. He was no ranter or raver. I could see how Powell had convinced somebody on our assignment desk to send a reporter out and hear his side of the story. But it was obvious that he had been taken in by Beter's paranoid view of world affairs.

I called the station from our truck after we had completed our interview. I told the desk there was no reason to use the tape on the air unless somebody wanted to make a laughingstock out of a decent man who had been hoodwinked into believing the missile story was the "real McCoy."

But a producer insisted that we microwave the interview back and then management would decide if the story was airworthy. So we beamed the interview back to base as ordered. After the beam in there was silence on the other end of the two way radio. The producers knew they had been had. Finally someone came on the radio and said, "Come on back in, we're not using the tape."

Some twenty years after the "bomb scare" no one has yet found any Russian nuclear devices in any Chicago area waterway. And it's likely no one will ever find them. Because they were never there in the first place.

THE HOSTAGE HOAX

As I groped around in the pre-dawn darkness, trying not to disturb my family, I knew it was going to be a hot and long day. The forecast had warned of steambath conditions. It was July 5, 1982, the day after a major holiday. It was a day you would want to spend in an air conditioned office. The summer doldrums had set in and on paper it should have been a quiet day from a news standpoint.

But when the phone rang around 4:30 A.M. I knew it was not my Aunt Matilda calling to inquire about my golf game. It was the assignment desk on the other end of the line, telling me to get into high gear and rendezvous with Steve Lasker and Bob Gadbois, a veteran mini-cam crew. Information was sketchy, the voice on the other end of the line said, but police had surrounded a west suburban Bloomingdale restaurant where a number of people were being held hostage. Time was of the essence so I didn't get a chance to wolf down a bowl of cereal or even a doughnut.

By the time we arrived at Mr. Memo's restaurant, it was just about daybreak and thirty-five policemen, with shotguns at the ready, had surrounded the building.

We were told that a thirty-year-old woman, the restaurant's assistant manager, was being held hostage by three or four men. The scenario began around three A.M., police said, when the woman called the restaurant owner at his home and said she was being held captive. We took up positions in a field across from the restaurant. It was an excellent vantage point because we had a clean shot to tape any action, if and when a swat team stormed the building.

It turned out to be a long siege. The sun came out and so did the humidity. It proved to be the hottest day of the summer with the mercury climbing well into the 90s. Our position was ideal from a camera standpoint but there was no shade for the TV crews, reporters, and spectators who had gathered to watch the unfolding drama. There was also no food and water available and reporters and TV crews couldn't risk leaving the scene. Sure as "God made green apples," if we did pull out for a few moments the cops would storm the restaurant. So we waited and waited. After several hours I began to "smell a rat." I got the feeling that nobody was in the building. It was obvious that police attempts to contact the invaders had proven fruitless. But at the same token I couldn't risk pulling out. I would have had "egg on my face" if the hostage incident turned out to be legit.

Although we had a clear view of the two and a half story building which was in a converted barn we were unable to cover the back door with a single crew. It was there we found out later, the woman who allegedly was being held captive had snuck out after she reportedly was able to free herself. That knocked out my theory that nobody was in the building but I still had my doubts that there were any bad guys inside.

The woman had left the building around 11:30 A.M. And was whisked off in a red van to a police command post for questioning.

The heat by then had begun to take it's toll. Two police officers, one from Roselle and one from Bloomingdale, suffered apparent heat stroke and were taken to Glendale Heights Hospital for treatment. Fortunately, an alert cameraman spotted a garden hose in the backyard of a nearby home. That enabled us to get some much needed water without pulling away from the scene. Going to the bathroom was not an issue since everybody had been sweating profusely for hours. No one needed to relieve themselves.

With the woman no longer in danger (there were no other hostages in the building, the assistant manager had told police) the DuPage County swat team, clad in green and brown fatigues, moved in. But before rushing the building the authorities made one more attempt to persuade the bad guys to surrender. They used a bullhorn, advising the intruders that they would not be harmed it they came out with their hands up. There was no response from inside.

Meanwhile the woman hostage had been telling investigators her version of what had happened. She claimed three or four men had entered Mr. Memo's at three A.M. while she was doing bookwork in the basement. According to the woman, the invaders demanded the combination to the safe, claiming they had come to the restaurant to collect a debt from the owner. Although she said she had been bound and gagged the woman told police, she had been able to free herself and called the restaurant owner at his home. The owner then called police who rushed to the scene. The woman alleged that she was able to sneak out a door when the intruders weren't looking.

Satisfied that there were no more hostages in the restaurant the swat team prepared to storm the building. A bomb technician placed a plastic device at the front door. Moments later a bomb blast rocked the neighborhood.

Wearing gas masks and armed to the teeth, the swat team entered the restaurant. They spent almost ninety minutes combing the building but found no trace of the intruders. DuPage County Sheriff Richard Doria told reporters, "there's nobody in there."

Although the hostage report turned out to be bogus television stations got some mileage out of the incident. The shots of the swat team rushing the restaurant, following the bomb blast, made all the evening TV newscasts in Chicago.

Phony hostage or not the affair proved to be an excellent training exercise to the swat team and the suburban police departments who were at the scene. And the publicity surrounding the story spurred other suburban departments into establishing special tactical units to deal with hostage or barricade situations.

After grilling the woman "hostage" authorities became convinced that she had fabricated the entire story. In other words, she wasn't tied up, the whole scenario was unfounded. They even gave the woman a lie detector test which confirmed the police view that the incident was a hoax. Bloomingdale Police Chief Patrick McMahon said the woman may have gotten into a situation that got way out of hand. The chief didn't elaborate what had gotten out of hand.

Several days after the incident police said they did not plan to file any charges against the assistant restaurant manager. Authorities apparently felt the woman had enough problems.

Some taxpayers though, weren't exactly enamored by the scenario. Costs for the operation were estimated at around two thousand dollars. That included overtime and fees for cops who had to be called in on their day off.

After spending several hours on the scene, my colleagues and myself felt that there was a smell of limburger to the hostage incident. We had come to the conclusion that there were no armed men inside. But you can't blame the cops for what they did. They had a witness who claimed she was being held captive. They had to play out the siege just like we did. They couldn't afford to take the chance that the whole thing was bogus.

But you learn something most every time. The moral of the story. If you are a reporter, don't leave your house or apartment without having some chow.

CHAPTER FOUR

The Chicago Chronicles

In late 1978 our general manager, Ed Joyce and the executive producer for news, Dick Goldberg sounded me out about doing three feature pieces a week for the station's one hour long six o'clock newscast. They informed me that if I accepted the feature proposition I would still be expected to continue my duties as a general assignment reporter.

At the time I was one of two reporters assigned to our "flagship newscast," the ten o'clock news. But Messrs. Joyce and Goldberg felt my new obligation would not interfere with my job as a reporter on hard news stories. They explained I would have a producer to help me set up the features and edit them. On rare occasions, they said, the producer could also write the pieces.

The producer turned out to be Dave Finney, a graduate of the University of Wisconsin and a television veteran. Dave was fun to work with and was and still is a very capable guy when it comes to the TV business.

But even with Finney's help I locked myself into some long hours. I would normally shoot and write my feature pieces in the morning and then go out on the street in the afternoon. I could have said no dice to the deal but the opportunity to have my own series proved too tempting.

I was given pretty much of a free hand on our feature series that we called the "Chicago Chronicles." As we explained on the air, you won't read about our Chronicle subjects in the Chicago guide books or travel brochures. Most of our Chronicle pieces dealt with people who weren't famous or pillars of society. They were average Joes. They would never be headliners or newsmakers. There were a few exceptions, but by and large most of our subjects were "unknowns."

Our Chicago Chronicle pieces ran anywhere from two minutes and twenty seconds to three minutes and fifteen seconds. That's a lot of time by local news standards. But if you are going to do stories of that kind you need time to develop the subject or character.

One of the reasons I enjoyed doing the Chronicles was that I had a free hand in selecting subjects. Executive producer Goldberg gave me carte blanche with just one exception. He insisted we do a piece on a Polish charwoman who worked nights in a loop office building scrubbing floors.

Dick had seen the movie "Call Northside 777," that was based on the true story of a Chicago man who had been sent to jail for a murder he did not commit. A newspaper reporter, played in the movie by Jimmie Stewart, uncovered new evidence and the innocent man was freed. The man, probably would have languished in prison all the rest of his life if it had not been for his mother.

She was a Polish woman who toiled as a charwoman, longing for the day her son would be a free man. She had placed an ad in a Chicago newspaper offering a reward for anyone who would come forward with information that would show her son was innocent. When somebody at the paper saw the ad they started working the story. The result a happy ending, Hollywood style.

Goldberg thought the yarn was the greatest thing since the invention of the internal combustion engine. He kept urging Finney and me to find a Polish charwoman who spent her nights on her hands and knees slaving away trying to make ends meet. Well, someone finally found us a charwoman all right and we went to do the story. We expected to see an elderly lady, pretty much on the heavy side. We were in for a rude awakening.

The charwoman we profiled was young, in her twenties. She looked like she had stepped out of *Vogue* magazine. Then to put frosting on the cake, she rarely got down on her hands and knees to scrub floors. She used a buffer instead. Our charwoman also cut quite a figure in her blue jump suit. The only thing she had in common with the charwoman who had worked so hard to clear her son's name was her Polish heritage.

We ran the piece on the new breed of charwomen and we never heard anymore from Goldberg on the subject of charwomen.

The "Chicago Chronicles" ran as a steady diet on our six o'clock news for almost two years. Then there was a change in management. The new brass felt that the station had too many features on the air. The Chronicles became a casualty. There were several revivals but the Chronicles never came back to Channel Two news on a thrice weekly basis. It was fun while it lasted.

THE NEWSIE

We launched our "Chicago Chronicle" series with a story about a newsie, a guy who made a living peddling papers from a newsstand. That's something of a vanishing breed these days.

When we ran into Joe Zeman in early 1979, he had been running a newsstand at the corner of LaSalle and Division for almost thirty years. Zeman, a short stubby guy, around fifty years old, grew up in the Depression and claimed he started hawking papers at the age of four.

By newsie standards, Joe Zeman had come a long way. His newsstand was almost posh, equipped with among other things, a phone, a big clock, a heater, and even carpeting. Most of Zeman's customers were regulars. Like clockwork they would stop each day to pick up a *Tribune* or *Sun-Times*. For his more discriminating clientele Zeman offered adult magazines, scratch sheets, and a wide assortment of comic books.

Zeman was a bear for wear. The newsstand was open seven days a week. And for all practical purposes Zeman's operation was a one man band. Joe though, apparently thrived on the marathon hours, summing up his work week this way: "Eat, sleep, work, eat, sleep, work."

Because Joe kept his nose to the grindstone, Zeman didn't have much time for social activity. His best pal, outside of his mother, was Bill Hodo who ran a shoe shine parlor across the street. Hodo also kept an eye on the newsstand when Zeman took one of his rare days off.

Unfortunately Hodo wasn't around the time a woman, posing as a customer, slipped a "Mickey" into Joe's coffee and then proceeded to take all the money from Joe's till. Joe later explained to me how the woman used a ruse in order to rob him.

The Newsie, Joe Zeman, operated a North Side newsstand for almost thirty years. He claimed he started hawking papers when he was just four years old.

"She comes up here, 'Joe I gotta cup of coffee, is that all right?' Real nice, real sweet, sweet talk, and so I says all right, thank you, that's very nice of you. I took the coffee innocently and so she stood as if she was waiting for the bus. Little by little, in a matter of minutes I was out."

When Joe woke up from his unscheduled doze, the woman was gone and so was Joe's money. The "Mickey Finn" had done it's job.

About a year and a half after Joe's incident with the "Mickey Finn," Zeman got zapped again. Joe and his newsstand were evicted from the site because a new supermarket was going to be built on the north side of Division Street.

Fortunately Joe's homeless status didn't last very long. Real estate magnate Arthur Rubloff and Jewel Foods, the operator of the supermarket, picked up the tab for a new stand on the southeast corner of LaSalle and Division. So all Joe had to do, it turned out, was to move across the street.

Zeman, though, had one more stumbling block to get over. A resident in a senior citizens high rise tried to block the move, claiming the newsstand would bring riff raff to the corner. But the elderly gentlemen who had complained about the stand couldn't convince anyone else that it was a problem. Zeman was home free.

Joe proved to be a good neighbor and even a good Samaritan to the folks in the high rise and there were no more complaints about Zeman and his newsstand. As for the senior citizen that Joe had called troublesome, that issue was soon settled. Zeman described what had happened very succinctly: "He's not around anymore. He kicked the bucket."

We don't know what happened to Joe. His newsstand as of the spring of 1997 was still at the corner. But there is never any sign of life. The stand is padlocked and a vending machine for the *Chicago Tribune* sits in front. We made some inquiries around the neighborhood but nobody seems to know anything as far as Zeman is concerned.

THE COURT BUFFS

You will see them every weekday at the Dirksen Federal Building in downtown Chicago. They come from all walks of life although most of them are retired now. They have one thing in common, an interest in the judicial process.

But to the lawyers, prosecutors, judges, and court personnel who work at the Federal building, they are known as the court buffs.

Anton Valukas, was the U.S. Attorney for the northern district of Illinois in the late 1980s. He prosecuted a number of high profile cases and in that capacity came under close scrutiny from the court buffs. His assessment of the buffs was very positive:

"They know what's good in the courtroom. They've seen all the arguments. They've seen us up there and they can tell you when you are on and when you are off."

You'll find the court buffs where the action is. Look for a juicy trial and the buffs will be there, savoring every word and every nuance. They keep an eagle eye on the Judge and the jury. They rarely miss a thing.

One longtime court buff was Louis Rubin who for years was a regular at the courthouse. Rubin claimed it was hard to pull the rug over the buffs' collective eyes:

"We can determine when a witness is lying by his facial expression and by the hesitations in his answers. I can say without hesitation that we are right about ninety eight per cent of the time."

The buffs gather each weekday morning at the Dirksen Building cafeteria where they map strategy over coffee and rolls. The buffs, primarily a male group, look over the courtroom calendar before deciding which case is worth spending some time on. Then they fan out to various courtrooms to see for themselves.

If the trial or hearing is boring, the buffs will move on. But usually the buffs are "right on the beam." They have a sixth sense in knowing which cases are newsworthy or good theater. If, on one of the few occasions that they strike out, the buffs will re-group their forces and stake out another courtroom.

Sometimes when there is a surprise guilty plea, hard hitting testimony, or a great cross examination, a buff will leave that courtroom and inform his colleagues who are somewhere else. Then the whole gang will descend on the courtroom where the "good stuff" is going on.

The buffs' assessments of various trials and the personalities involved are reported in the *Courtwatchers Newsletter.* The newsletter, edited by buff Roy Suzuki, a former IRS agent, is eagerly awaited by those who ply their trade at the Federal Building.

The newsletter, on a scale of one to ten rates the efforts of prosecutors, defense lawyers, and even judges. The newsletter also has other tidbits, including predictions on the outcome of trials, background information on the participants, and courtroom gossip. The rating system is similar to the way debate judges rank high school and college debaters.

A typical rating was published in the October 16, 1986 issue of the newsletter. The case involved then state representative Lawrence Bullock of Chicago who was standing trial on corruption charges. The Buffs not only rated the performance of the lawyers during their closing arguments but also timed the length of their presentations as well.

NAME OF ATTORNEY	TIME	RATING
Joe Duffy, Prosecutor	*1 hr. 49 min.*	*9.0*
Sam Adam, Defense	*2 hrs. 30 min.*	*8.5*
Candace Fabri, Prosecutor	*1 hr. 17 min.*	*9.5*

The "shadow jury," as the court buffs call themselves predicted that Bullock would be found guilty. The buffs, in their newsletter, wrote that prosecutor Duffy's "brilliant cross examination of

Bullock had doomed him." The buffs were right, Bullock was convicted.

Jurors don't go unscathed either. The newsletter sometimes assesses jurors as to their demeanor, garb, body shape, intelligence or lack thereof. This is how the court buffs sized up a Federal jury that was hearing a case where a Chicago circuit court Judge was on trial.

Juror no. one: male age 25, loner, serious. Juror no. two: female age 35, bored, talkative, sometimes sleeps during testimony. Juror no. three: female age 60, glasses, serious, intelligent. Juror no. four: male age 45, pot belly, glasses, jokes, reads newspapers.

Juror no. five: female age 35, nicely dressed. Bored, dozing sleeping, sexy, talkative chews gum. Juror no. six: male age 40, pot bellied, serious, astute-looking, possible foreman, casual dress, wears expensive cowboy boots.

The newsletter went on with more detailed descriptions of jurors sitting in the second row. The entire jury was described as a "wage earner" jury.

The newsletter also gives heavy play to key witnesses in high profile cases. Their appearance on the stand is reported the way fan magazines describe their favorite stars:

"At 3:48 P.M. A bombshell witness in the form of Irwin Weiner, a short, stocky, balding, gray haired man weighing about 170 pounds appeared on behalf of one of the defendants."

Just about every word uttered by Weiner on both direct examination and cross examination was reported in the newsletter. But the newsletter, most always very accurate in predicting the outcome of trials, was way off the mark in forecasting that Weiner was going to be hit in the near future. From the newsletter of March 25, 1983:

"It was the gruesome opinion of some of the veteran court watchers that Irwin Weiner will never enjoy his 70th birthday."

The newsletter then listed a number of men who had been slain in gangland style, indicating that Weiner's name would be added to the necrology. Weiner, a street smart bail bondsman, was sixty six years old when his demise was predicted. However, Irv never ran afoul of crime syndicate torpedoes. He lived until he was eighty years old. Weiner died of natural causes.

When a well known defense attorney or a hot shot prosecutor goes into high gear the courtroom is S.R.O.

That was the case when New York lawyer Bruce Cutler came to Chicago to defend a crime syndicate figure. Here's an excerpt from the Nov. 9, 1991 newsletter:

"Before a packed house, the long awaited appearance of Bruce Cutler (John Gotti's mouthpiece) commenced at 2:41 P.M.....Bruce came into the Dirksen like gangbusters...Bruce unloaded his Brooklyn style of jury persuasion on the curious jurors and court-watchers...

"Benito" Cutler caps his remarks with a showmanship touch in appropriate situations...You've got to see and hear him perform."

The buffs gave Cutler his "Benito" moniker because of his shaved heard and bombastic style. Despite the impression that Cutler made on the buffs and other spectators, his client was convicted.

Courtroom oratory isn't the only thing that impresses the buffs. Defense attorney Jo-Anne Wolfson was praised for her skillful cross examination of a key government witness. But Wolfson also got kudos from the "shadow jury" because of other factors. From the Nov. 9, 1991 newsletter:

"She (Wolfson) was dressed to kill in a jumper black Outfit, big silver buckle, black leather high heeled boots, and a gray sports coat. She looks 45 years old but is 57 years old."

Prosecutors get their share of praise, too. The buffs gave assistant U.S. Attorney Julian Solotorovsky high marks in the March 20, 1985 newsletter:

"Big Julian Solotorovsky starts his rebuttal argument by using a novel, creative, and ingenious opening. Boom! He makes a dramatic statement that puts the monkey on the back of the jurors...Just like Maestro Solti, Solotorovsky orchestrated a truly great rebuttal overture. He started off with a bang and ended with a crescendo."

Federal Judge Prentice Marshall, always had a soft spot in his heart for the buffs. For years he hosted an annual luncheon for the group. An event relished by all of the participants, especially the judge.

"I think they're a great bunch of human beings. They're retired gentlemen...They've paid their dues. They've worked hard. They've lived productive, honest lives. They are interested in government. They are interested in justice."

Judge Marshall is not alone in his admiration for the buffs. Prosecutors and defense attorneys alike go out of their way to chat with them. But the motive is different. They want the buffs' opinion about their performance.

I've been in the hallway outside of courtrooms during a trial recess when I've observed attorneys collaring the buffs. Often the conversation goes like this: "How did I do? What do you think of my arguments? How did the witness stand up to my cross examination?"

But time for true confessions. I, too have collared the buffs to get their views, particularly a prediction of a jury verdict. Their crystal balls have a high accuracy rate and when I repeated those predictions on the air, I looked like I was quite a prophet too.

LIBONATI

There are few, if any politicians who would allow a newspaper photographer to take his or her picture sitting with public enemy number one. But, that did happen in Chicago in 1931. Roland Libonati not only posed with Al Capone but told me later that he would have done it again.

Imagine what would happen in this day and age of political correctness. Imagine what a field day that columnists and TV commentators would have over such an incident. The politician would be figuratively boiled in oil, his or her career as a public servant would be over.

However, it didn't hurt Libonati who was serving in the Illinois legislature at the time. He not only ran successfully for re-election but later ended up in Congress.

In a 1974 interview with Libonati, "Libby," as his friends called him, told me about the famous Wrigley Field visit with Capone. Libonati says he was sitting in the stands with the then governor of Illinois when he was summoned by one of Capone's minions to meet with "Big Al." Capone had brought his son to the game.

"I went to speak to his son who had a desire to become a lawyer. Capone was an admirer of mine and because I was a young lawyer, it impressed him."

Libonati said that legendary Cubs catcher Gabby Hartnett approached the three who were sitting in the first row of box seats. Then a photographer arrived on the scene. According to Libonati, there were some other dignitaries seated near Capone but, they scattered when the "photog" started clicking away. Roland said he had no intention of embarrassing Capone.

59

"I wouldn't do that to my friend who I respected and he respected me."

Roland Libonati speaks to veterans at the Daley Center. "Libby" was a controversial lawmaker who had his picture taken with Al Capone.

LibonatI's reputed ties to organized crime never hurt him at the ballot box. He was first elected to the Illinois house in 1928, became a member of the state Senate in 1940, and eventually ended up in the halls of Congress, serving as a representative from Chicago's Seventh District.

While in Springfield, he was a leader of what was known as the "West Side Bloc," a group of lawmakers who consistently opposed crime bills sponsored by the Chicago Crime Commission.

Although Libonati was dubbed "Mr. Malaprop" because of his flowery but somewhat tangled oratory he was no buffoon. I say that after profiling Libonati on several occasions and being involved with him in a number of veterans day affairs.

After he left Congress Libonati would often go the "hall," which is the way the pols describe Chicago's City Hall. Libonati had a certain ritual he would go through when he arrived at the building. He would meet and greet pols, ward heelers, and bureaucrats who were usually milling around in the lobby. "Libby," his hands outstretched would address most everyone the same, "How's it going, good to see you."

Oh, he was a politician of the old school all right. But, behind that hail fellow, well met veneer was a pretty shrewd politician.

He once polled eighty percent of the votes cast in a race for a Congressional seat. Granted it was a safe seat for a Democrat, granted he had the backing of the regular Democratic organization, and granted he had the support of the Mob, but the people in his district genuinely liked Libonati.

"Libby" got a lot of heat over allegations that he was the Chicago Outfit's representative in Washington. However, Libonati's voting record was considered progressive when it came to social legislation. While in Congress he helped win passage of the civil rights act of 1964.

Libonati never forgot his humble roots. He came out of a poor neighborhood on Chicago's west side but ended up with a Bachelor's degree from the University of Michigan and a diploma from Northwestern Law School. Roland said there were others from his neck of the woods who lived the American dream:

"I've seen men come up from that area that had no chance at all. They became successful men, bankers, lawyers, doctors, professional men. Only in this country could that happen."

Libonati could never shake off allegations that he was the Chicago Mob's man in Washington. Cynics said that after the crime syndicate wanted new blood in Washington, Libonati was ordered in 1964, by then Mob boss Sam Giancana to give up his Congressional seat. Libonati added fuel to the fire by not seeking re-election. Observers who were close to the scene believe Libonati threw in the towel rather than face the wrath of the Mob hierarchy. But Libonati always claimed it was financial considerations and not any Mob edict that caused him to leave Washington. At any rate he returned to Chicago and resumed the practice of law.

It was then that "Libby" a World War I Doughboy turned his attention to veterans affairs. He soon played a prominent role with the American Legion.

Every November 11th, Veterans Day would find Libonati giving a stem winding but long oration. Then he would head to the

Bismarck Inn where he would regale his cronies, over lunch, with a wide variety of stories.

Often he would call me, asking if I would emcee some Legion function. I had a very busy schedule but "Libby" was quite an arm twister. More often than not I'd end up on the podium with Libby.

Once Libonati started speaking he could go on forever. I'll never forget one incident at the Daley Center when "Libby" was really wound up. Dignitaries became concerned because the program was geared for the traditional playing of taps in front of the eternal flame at exactly eleven o'clock. It was at eleven A.M. on November 11,1918 that the guns became silent, ending World War I.

By 10:50 A.M. Libonati had shown no signs of slowing down, it was obvious he was going on seemingly forever. Fortunately one brave Legionnaire discreetly came up to Libonati and reminded him that everyone had to assemble outside quickly if the eleven o'clock deadline was to be met. Libonati halted his oration and everything went according to "Hoyle."

Father Time finally caught up to Libonati in 1991. He succumbed to the realities of old age. He was ninety when he died.

You won't find politicians of the Libonati mold around anymore. Some will say he was a dinosaur, a throwback to an unenlightened age when Machine politicians called the shots. That may be. But, from a reportorial standpoint I miss covering stories about characters like Libonati. Most politicians of today are a bland lot with every move and word dictated by image conscious advisors or public relations firms.

Say what you want about Libonati but he didn't come from that mold!

WALLY THE WIRETAPPER

Walter Dewey Pritchard was a longtime Chicago gumshoe who was best known by the sobriquet of "Wally the Wiretapper." Pritchard got the moniker because of his penchant for tape recording phone conversations. But Wally spent more time "painting the town red" than keeping his nose to the grindstone. He was a real "Rush Street cowboy," a Damon Runyon type character, who loved the bright lights.

Pritchard used to pick up some loose change by serving as a bodyguard for Mobsters. However Wally achieved his greatest notoriety when he was heard on tape boasting that he was the crime syndicate's dog hit man.

Wally's escapades often got him into trouble with the law. Soon he was getting his mail at places like Sandstone, Minnesota; Milan, Michigan; Oxford, Wisconsin; and Marion, Illinois. Those fair communities, in case you didn't know, are all home to Federal prisons.

One of Wally's sojourns at Sandstone was the result of using walkie talkies at a Miami racetrack to report race results to some of his cronies. The cronies, in turn would then call Chicago and place bets on the race before bookies in the "Windy City" knew the race results. That was strictly a no-no.

Pritchard loved to play the cabaret scene. In fact he first attracted the attention of the FBI in the 1960s when he was seen hobnobbing with Mob figure Manny Skar in Rush Street bars. Skar was gunned down in 1965 at a time when Wally was serving as Skar's bodyguard. Pritchard incidentally wasn't around the night that Skar met his demise.

Wally Pritchard at the Dirksen Federal Building.
Pritchard — a Damon Runyon type character — denied he
was the crime syndicate's "dog hit man."

Wally was a great storyteller, but was always tight-lipped about his associates in the underworld. Even after consuming a half-dozen martinis, which was a daily ritual, Pritchard wouldn't talk out of school about any of his Mob friends.

But Wally's mouth got him into trouble on more than one occasion. Pritchard once boasted that he was known as the official dog hit man because he killed four dogs during a burglary. Wally didn't know it, but his braggadocio was recorded for posterity. Unbeknownst to "Wally the Wiretapper," the man he told the story to, John Forbes, was a government informer. Forbes was wearing a concealed tape recorder.

In my conversations with Wally, Pritchard always denied being involved in any canine capers. As he put it: "the only thing I ever killed was a cockroach." Despite his many denials Pritchard was stuck with the dog hit man nickname for many years.

You'd see Wally hanging around his favorite haunts in Chicago and then before you knew it he would be wearing prison denims again. He was back at Sandstone in 1984 after being convicted of wire fraud and illegal possession of eavesdropping equipment. Sandstone, located in northern Minnesota, is hardly the place to spend the winter months.

Wally was a helluva jailhouse lawyer, often filing lawsuits that protested the food or conditions of the prison in which he was residing. But his complaints fell on deaf ears.

Wally had a habit of getting into hot water when he was in the hoosegow. We visited Wally one frigid January day at Sandstone only to find that Pritchard was on bad paper with the warden. Prison officials had found escape paraphernalia in Wally's cell area. Pritchard ended up doing hard time in the prison's segregation unit.

He once did a stretch at the Marion Federal prison in southern Illinois. Wally wasn't in the maximum security unit but in a separate facility or camp for inmates who were not prone to violent crimes. But the lure of the bright lights proved to be irresistible. Pritchard walked away from the camp and went on the lam. It didn't take long for the authorities to catch up with our famous gumshoe. The FBI spotted Wally hoisting martinis in the bar of a south suburban hotel in Oak Lawn. It was back to jail for Pritchard.

Wally finally got out of jail in 1989 and vowed to go straight. He enrolled in a twenty month electronics course at the Devry Institute of Technology in Chicago.

A wiretapper taking an electronics course? Well, Wally said he had lots to learn. Pritchard said his new motto was "say no to bugs." According to Pritchard, he was going to help people find bugs rather than plant them.

In February of 1992, Wally was in one of his favorite haunts, the Bel Air Lounge, on Chicago's North Side. It was there that he was fatally stricken with a heart attack. It was probably the way Wally would have wanted to go.

Ironically the sixty-four-year-old Pritchard was due in court the day after he died. Chicago Police had caught him driving a stolen car that was filled with what the cops said were burglary tools. Wally told us shortly before he died that it was no big deal. He said he was going to beat the criminal charges against him. Pritchard remained the eternal optimist to the end.

Perhaps Federal Judge Nicholas Bua summed up Wally's character the best when he sentenced him on racketeering charges some years back. Said Bua, "I see no redeeming features for Mr. Pritchard at all, except that he is a nice guy."

THE POLICE REPORTER

While most of the city slept, Joe Cummings would be on the prowl in his fire engine red Chevy Impala. Cummings' police scanner would constantly be barking out the jargon of police and fire dispatchers, 10'-1's, 10-50s, and 2-11's.

For twelve years Cummings worked the overnight shift, as a police reporter, for WBBM Newsradio 78 in Chicago. His beat took him all over the city from the Gold Coast on the North Side to the huge public housing projects that dotted the South and West Sides. Toiling through the wee hours, Cummings would run across his share of characters in his job as a radio reporter. But Cummings was as colorful as some of the Damon Runyon types that he covered on his beat.

Cummings didn't get into broadcasting through the usual route. At a time when many working journalists had masters degrees, Cummings didn't even have a high school diploma.

Cummings was born in Cleveland, Ohio just as the great depression began sending the U.S. economy into a tailspin. Joe says his father was murdered shortly before he was born and that his mother died two years later. For a time Cummings lived with a great aunt but later spent his formative years in an orphanage. The military seemed like a way out, so Cummings, as a teen-ager, joined the navy to see the world. Cummings said he was a gob for three and a half years before being discharged in the spring of 1951. In 1955, Cummings said, he was working on a great lakes ore boat that made a pit stop in Chicago. He's been in the "Windy City" ever since.

Joe liked the sauce when he was a young man and by the time he was working as a short order cook at a North Side greasy spoon he was drinking heavily. He literally hit the skids, ending up as a Madison Street wino. The story might have ended right there, but for Monsignor Ignatius McDermott. "Father Mac," as the affable clergyman is known to his skid row parishioners, came across Joe and set him on the straight and narrow. Cummings says he hasn't had a drink in forty years.

Cummings gets the lowdown on a 1979 fire from a Chicago Police Officer.

He got his start in journalism as a photographer for the Southtown Economist, a suburban newspaper. That whetted his appetite. So Joe became a scribe for the City News Bureau, a training round for aspiring journalists. Cummings' three year stint (1961-64) with the City News Bureau launched his career as a police reporter. He was about ten years older than most of his colleagues at CNB. The average CNB employee is a young man or woman just out of college and eager to set the world of journalism on fire.

Although Cummings lacked a B.A. or even a GED, he had a lot of street sense. Cummings soon found out he had excellent rapport with cops and firefighters. He was on his way.

Cummings happened to be in the right place at the right time. In the early 60s, radio station managers began to realize there was money in local news. They started to beef up their news departments. Cummings caught on at WNUS which was the first all news radio station in Chicago. When WNUS went belly up, Cummings landed with WCFL, a rock and roll station, which had a strong news department. Cummings reporting attracted the attention of the brass at CBS-owned WBBM. In May of 1968 WBBM became an all news operation. Before long Cummings joined the payroll.

Cummings soon became the overnight man at the station. It was a marriage made in heaven! Joe loved roaming the city, covering fires, gambling raids, homicides, and whatnot. Cummings had a ringside seat at the city's underbelly reporting on the Richard Speck case, the 1968 riots, and the 1975 murder of Mob boss Sam Giancana. Speck was convicted of murdering 8 student nurses at a South Side town house in 1966. It was called "the crime of the century." Cummings who has seen his share of corpses described, the slayings as the "worst murder scene he had ever seen."

Cummings has eaten his share of smoke too, tromping over fire hoses, wading through puddles, facing sometimes blast furnace heat as he did radio reports from the fire scene.

One cold winter night, in March of 1979, we ran across Cummings reporting from the scene of a raging apartment house fire in the 32-hundred block of North Pulaski. It was an extra alarm blaze, a 2-11, which is a two bagger in a firefighters nomenclature. Cummings in a fur hat and storm coat was interviewing a battalion chief, garnering an update for a fire that had caused considerable property damage. Cummings ended his report, his voice rising to be heard over the din of fire trucks that were beginning to pull away. He gave his signature closing, "I'm Joe Cummings reporting from the North Side."

It was about two A.M. when we followed Joe to his favorite eatery, Miller's Pub, one of the few restaurants in the loop that is open in the wee hours of the morning. When Cummings worked the night shift he most always stopped at Miller's to recharge his batteries. More often than not, Joe would gobble down a big steak in the process. Miller's Pub, operated by the popular Gallios brothers, has a colorful clientele and sometimes Cummings was able to come away with information that paid off newswise.

Cummings said that at one time he got tired of toiling all night, it didn't give him much of a social life. So he asked management if he could try days. They obliged but Cummings found out that his free wheeling style didn't mesh with normal duty hours. He soon was back on a more bohemian schedule. As Cummings explained: "I nearly went crazy. I'm used to getting from one side of the city to the other in ten minutes. When I got put on days it took me ten minutes to get across Michigan Avenue at Erie. I mean, the crowds, the people, the traffic. I'm not use to that. So I asked to go back on nights. I mean nights is where the action is."

Cummings was always able to get along with the police. Detectives knew if they told Joe something in confidence, the veteran radio reporter would keep his mouth shut about it. As Cummings put it: "I think one of the highest compliments I get is when I walk up to the scene and I'll say Joe Cummings WBBM and the cop will say 'Don't talk to him, he is a reporter' and the other guy will say, 'He's one of us,' to me that's a compliment."

His police contacts did pay off. According to Cummings, he broke the story of the murder of Sam Giancana. The Giancana hit was one of the big stories of the year back in 1975. But long hours and the graveyard shift finally took it's toll on Cummings. In March of 1980 he collapsed while covering a firemen's union ratification meeting at McCormick Place. Cummings who was forty nine underwent bypass surgery. That was followed with a bout with gallstones and some more heart problems. It put the thirty mark on Cummings' career as a newsman.

Cummings left WBBM and ended up on the city payroll, courtesy of then Mayor Jane Byrne. That was a patronage job and when Harold Washington became mayor in 1983, Cummings' days at City Hall were numbered. For a while Joe labored in private industry working the phones for a north suburban appliance store. He finally tired of that and retired.

If Cummings' health had stood up he'd still be cruising the city at night chasing fire engines and squad cars. But for a fellow who once wanted to be a policeman Cummings did the next best thing to actually wearing a badge and packin' a snub nosed thirty eight. As it turned out, Cummings probably saw more bodies, bank jobs, and rumbles than most cops do in a lifetime.

ROSS CASCIO

Ross Cascio never hit a big league home run, never held elective office and never designed any of the famous skyscrapers that dot the Chicago skyline. Yet Cascio, a Chicago character if there ever was one, probably for a time was as well known as any ball player, alderman, or architect. Cascio was even the inspiration for a popular Steve Goodman ballad, "The Lincoln Park Pirates," that was on the charts for a while in the 1970s.

Cascio was a long time tow truck operator who started playing "Captain Hook" with cars back in 1960. For twenty one years Cascio's fleet of trucks roamed around the North Side hooking cars that were parked on private property. The burly Cascio, never the diplomatic type, ran the Lincoln Towing Service. Ross' firm hit a raw nerve with motorists who claimed he was guilty of what they called vehicular piracy. Soon Cascio became the town heavy getting berated by both newspaper columnists and aldermen. But Cascio told me he didn't mind the bad ink. Ross took it in stride claiming the publicity was good for business:

"All the derogatory statements they made in the news media, it sold newspapers, but I'm still towing cars…I got press out of it. It's something that built my business."

Cascio and other tow truck operators filled a need on the North Side, particularly in the Lincoln Park, Old Town, and the high rise belt along Lake Shore Drive where parking space is limited. Visitors to those area frequently would park their vehicles on private property or worse yet block driveways. Some inconsiderate motorists would take spaces or stalls reserved for tenants or customers of small retail shops that were located in the neighborhood.

So Cascio would get calls from irate landlords or businessmen asking him to remove cars that were on their property. Cynics said that there was more to it than that. They claimed that there was a sweetheart deal between Cascio and his clients. The property owners, the cynics said, would get a kickback from Cascio for each car that was towed.

Cascio's heavy handed tactics touched off a whirlwind of complaints. Motorists said that their cars were being damaged when towed. Others claimed Lincoln Towing had hooked their cars even if they were legally parked on public property. Still others beefed about strong arm methods saying they were threatened with physical harm by Cascio and his employees.

Cascio wouldn't accept checks or credit cards from motorists who came to his fortress like office on Fullerton Avenue to retrieve their vehicles. It was cash on the barrelhead. The tariff was twenty five dollars in the late 1960s. The price was jacked up as time went on. If the hapless motorist couldn't come up with the towing fee, the vehicle owner would end up paying additional costs for storage. Ross' employees were often surly and treated many customers with rudeness.

Ross was no "Mr. Rogers" type and enjoyed intimidating his patrons. At one time he kept a big mean, German Shepherd chained to the wall near his desk. A billy club, a blackjack, and a baseball bat were all within easy reach of Cascio. Cascio even installed bullet proof glass in his office which was protected by a steel door. Cascio contended the security was necessary to prevent mayhem from being committed on himself and his staff. As he explained:

"If we didn't have the security we have here, we'd have employees being shot, because we have people coming in here who are awfully vicious."

Cascio went on to tell me that some of his customers didn't always act like ladies and gentlemen. Some, he said vented their anger in the outer office by defecating or urinating on the floor. He said some came armed and fired shots into his office while others, he said, apparently in blind rages, drove their cars into the Lincoln Towing Company front gate.

Ross Cascio — controversial towing firm operator. His firm's activities spawned a popular fok song, "The Lincoln Park Pirates."

When Lincoln relocated farther north to a site on North Clark Street, Cascio installed a six inch steel I beam to give his front gate a little protective armor. Once when visiting Lincoln Towing, Ross showed me a Chevy Monte Carlo that had a recent joust with the beefed up front gate. The Monte Carlo definitely came out second best.

It was inevitable that somebody would be seriously injured or even killed in an altercation between motorists and towing company employees. And in fact, it did happen. Two persons did die. One a motorist and the other a worker for a towing company, not Lincoln.

Although nobody was killed or even seriously injured in confrontations with Ross and his staff, Cascio was soon spending time in court defending his firm in a number of lawsuits. One plaintiff, asking for five million dollars, charged he was confronted with rudeness and intimidation when he attempted to get his car out of hock. In another case, a Federal court ordered Cascio to pay some twenty seven thousand dollars in damages to a suburban chemist who had testified that he and two friends were beaten and stabbed by Lincoln Towing employees when they tried to reclaim their cars.

Cascio's problems were compounded by the IRS and a divorce settlement. Uncle Sam claimed Ross owed forty six thousand dollars in back taxes. Cascio ended up filing for bankruptcy.

Even though Ross and Lincoln Towing fell on bad times, Cascio was a survivor. He bounced back and stayed in business. But Lincoln and all the towing companies had come under close scrutiny by the city and the Illinois Commerce Commission. New regulations were imposed and some of the abuses in the industry were eliminated.

Cascio remained in business until 1981 when he sold Lincoln Towing Service to a suburban man. There were reports that Ross still had a piece of the action at Lincoln Towing, but he denied it. Cascio said he had hung up his tow trucks forever.

In retirement Ross was plagued by ill health. He suffered two heart attacks and a third proved fatal. He was sixty years old when he died in 1987.

Ross Cascio engaged in tough business practices. There's no doubt about that. He was rough hewn all right. However, I think his bark was a little bit bigger than his bite. He enjoyed being perceived in the media as a villain. But like Cascio or not, towing companies are a necessary evil. If they didn't exist people would park their cars wherever they felt like it.

So the next time you get hemmed in by an illegally parked car you might just say, "Ross where are you when we need you!"

THE MAYOR OF RUSH STREET

There have been many pretenders to the throne but in our corner there has been only one "Mayor of Rush Street," a guy by the name of Maury Kahn. The title of course is strictly honorary. For readers not familiar with Chicago, Rush Street is located on the Near North Side and has long been a favorite of conventioneers, tourists, singles and suburbanites. It's an area filled with bars and restaurants. A section of the city where visitors and locals alike come to have a good time.

There have been others, through the years, who have been labeled the "Mayor of Rush Street." In some circles the late sportscaster Harry Carey, a bon vivant if there ever was one, had been described as the "Mayor of Rush Street." And Harry could certainly have made a strong bid for the crown. But when it came to knowing the "Great White Way" like the back of your hand, Maury Kahn had it over everyone else.

Kahn in the 1960s and 70s published a weekly magazine, "Nightlife in Chicago," that devoted much of it's space to the Rush Street scene. Although critics of the magazine called it a rag, Kahn claimed his publication enabled "visiting firemen" to know where the action was.

Maury even had a column in his magazine called "Maury Kahn Tells It Like It Is." Kahn went to bat for a number of causes in his column ranging from legalized prostitution to environmental protection. But editorial content was outweighed by the large number of ads that listed night clubs featuring strip teasers. The magazine most always had a picture of a busty exotic dancer on the cover. The exotic, more often than not, was a featured artist at a Rush Street area nightclub. "Nightlife" was distributed to area hotels where copies were grabbed up like hotcakes by conventioneers looking for an exciting night on the town.

Kahn, one night, gave this writer and a Channel Two News crew a guided tour of the Rush Street area. Mind you, this was in the mid 70s and the Street had changed considerably since it's glory days. Kahn was certainly the right man to give us the low down on Glitter Gulch. Maury had strong credentials to be a tour guide. Except for a hitch in the navy during World War II and a short stay as an involuntary guest in one of Uncle Sam's "bastilles," Maury had been a regular on the Rush Street scene since 1938.

As we walked along Rush Street on an early spring evening, Kahn lamented the passing of such famed night spots as the Club Alabam, The Living Room, The Tradewinds, The Cloister Inn, The Colony, The Scotch Mist, and of more recent vintage, Mr. Kelly's.

I remember stopping at The Tradewinds back in the 1950s. You even had to wear a tie to get into the cocktail lounge. But that was par for the course in those kind of places in that distant era. I didn't want to bring up anything unpleasant about the place to Maury but, the operator of The Tradewinds, a fellow by the name of Art

Adler, ended up in the city's sewer system. Adler, apparently had gotten on bad paper with some crime syndicate honchos who had him killed. The murder of Art Adler has never been solved.

Maury and I dropped into The Singapore which a decade earlier had been a gathering spot for celebrities of all sorts. Sports stars, entertainers, politicians, Mobsters, and even bluebloods were regulars at the Rush Street eatery. Frank Sinatra liked the cole slaw so much that the restaurant used to ship the stuff to Sinatra's residence in the Palm Springs area.

But the Singapore was no longer a steak and chop house. And it was no longer a must stop for celebrities when they visited Chicago. By the early 1970s the onetime Rush Street landmark was billing itself as The Singapore Show Lounge.

A big ad in Kahn's magazine touted an all star exotic revue that was being featured at the night spot. The ad boasted that the revue had gorgeous brunettes, luscious blondes, and dynamic redheads. When Kahn and I made our pilgrimage to The Singapore the main attraction was a stripper who billed herself as Susan Haze, the Fire Queen. It was a far cry from the time that the likes of Jimmy Durante, Jack E. Leonard, Mickey Mantle, and Rhonda Fleming would flock to The Singapore for it's signature bill of fare, the barbecued ribs.

The Singapore eventually went the way of the wreckers ball and with it went the last vestiges of the old Rush Street.

But as Maury Kahn pointed out that spring night, Rush Street had survived both good and bad times, lows and highs. Like the old gray mare Rush Street "ain't what it used to be." But, then again, there are those who say the change is for the better.

Singles bars, trendy restaurants, an upscale hotel, and even a department store have replaced the plethora of clip joints that flourished for a time. As one bar owner told the *Chicago Tribune,* "Rush Street is unique and if the city ever loses it, we will lose something special."

THE COMIC WHO COULDN'T LAUGH ANYMORE

He was hardly a show business legend but for years Benny Dunn was a fixture on the Chicago night club scene. Benny first toiled as a comedian, then as a night club emcee, and finally as a public relations man for Hugh Hefner's Playboy empire.

Dunn who looked like a poor man's Rodney Dangerfield once had aspirations of being a top banana. But Benny claimed a stint in the army during World War II changed all that. Benny said one of his duties was to entertain wounded GIs at McCloskey hospital in Temple, Texas. Dunn said that visiting wards filled with battlefield casualties made it tough for him to go back to the pratt fall and slapstick routine. Dunn claimed he was really funny before his army hitch and that he had every intention of resuming his career as a comedian when he was discharged.

Shortly after shedding his O.D.'s for civilian garb, Dunn said, his agent got him a gig at the old Morrison Hotel in the loop. According to Dunn when he got up on the stage of the Terrace Room he couldn't get funny and actually froze:

"I walked off the stage. I didn't know what was happening. I walked out of the room and out of the hotel and never entertained again."

Although Benny said his army experience soured him on cracking jokes, Benny stayed in show business as an emcee and night club manager. He worked in such well known night spots as the Black Orchid and the Trade Winds. Because of the rotund Dunn's poker face on stage friends began calling him "the Ed Sullivan of Rush Street."

When television began taking a toll on live nightclub acts Dunn rolled with the punches and got into public relations. Before long Benny caught on with Playboy where he once described himself as "the world's greatest gofer." In his Playboy days Benny hobnobbed with a lot of movie stars and other show business types. He soon became a man about town always trying to pitch a story or an item about Playboy to newspaper columnists.

To my knowledge Benny never married. His whole life, at least in his later years, revolved around his aging mother Rose. Rose Dunn, better known as "Mama Dunn," was something of a legend among entertainers and had been a "godmother" to many of the show business crowd in Chicago.

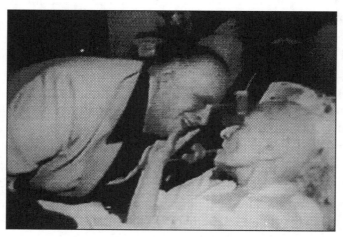

Benny Dunn visits his ailing mother Rose "Mamma" Dunn.

"Mama Dunn," a bundle of energy, suffered a stroke that left her hospitalized and partially paralyzed. Dunn was a constant companion at his mother's bedside spending almost every waking hour there. Before long it got to the point that Benny was putting in more time at the hospital than at his office. That didn't set too well with his supervisors at Playboy. They complained he was rarely showing up for work. Benny got the ax.

It was all downhill for Benny after that. He was forced to move into a second rate apartment. His health began to deteriorate. "Mama Dunn" never recovered from that stroke and was never able to go back home. When she died Benny was devastated. His mother's passing took a terrible toll on Dunn and it wasn't long after that Benny himself died.

Benny could be a real pain in the rear end sometimes. He would often call when you were on deadline rehashing some story or some request that had been made time and time again. If you don't believe me just ask a few columnists around town that knew Benny.

But give the guy credit when credit was due. Dunn was a colorful character who knew the Chicago nightclub scene. And to his dying day he never cared for the way the Rush Street district was changing. Dunn was from the old school who didn't like the trendy restaurants and bars catering to yuppies that had replaced the nightclubs with garish signs and 26 girls.

"It doesn't have the excitement, the old excitement anymore," Benny would lament.

And few, if any of Benny's generation would disagree with him on that.

VINCE GERACI

Vince Geraci had a knack of antagonizing a lot of powerful people. Before he left town Vince had made enemies with City Hall, the Chicago Police Department, the Cook County States Attorneys Office, the Mob, and even certain community groups.

Geraci was a big man in the massage parlor game when the rub down palaces were in their heyday in the 1970s. Geraci started small, opening an adult book store called The Haven. It was located in the Edgebrook community on Chicago's far North Side and soon became a center of controversy in that neck of the woods.

Geraci got the bright idea of putting a massage parlor in the back of the book store. He hired a number of attractive young women to work as masseuses. But Vince's masseuses had nothing in common with Andy Lotshaw, the old Cubs rub down expert who used to massage the aching muscles of Cubs hitters and pitchers. What Geraci was doing was strictly illegal because there was a city ordinance on the books at the time prohibiting public massage by members of the opposite sex. That didn't stop Geraci who argued that the ordinance was unconstitutional. Vince was buying time hoping that a long drawn out court fight would enable him to keep operating until a ruling by the Illinois Supreme Court would shut him down for good.

Geraci soon had a gold mine on his hands. He opened two more massage parlors all called The Haven. Clients flocked to Geraci's establishments where they were massaged by young women who were topless when they went about their business.

One night cameraman Steve Lasker and myself convinced Geraci that a television story about The Haven would be good for business. Geraci no shrinking violet when it came to publicity agreed. The then news director at Channel Two didn't need much convincing. He thought it was a wonderful idea. He believed that an inside look at a massage parlor might help boost our then dismal ratings.

Massage parlor hostess Clarabelle talks to a prospective client.

We ended up filming the Geraci story at his parlor that was on the Near North Side. We picked the noon hour on a week day which we thought might be a dead time. We were in for a real surprise. The place was doing a land office business. Men, both young and old, many garbed in business suits were waiting in the vestibule to be summoned by their favorite masseuse.

Clarabelle, Geraci's hostess, was busy on the phone explaining The Haven's policies to potential customers. We filmed Clarabelle's end of the conversation which went like this:

"Yes, sir I'll be glad to explain to you the parties and principles of The Haven massage parlor. Our girls are topless. You may touch them from the waist up."

Clarabelle's brief but frank sales pitch was very effective. The phone never seemed to stop ringing and customers kept arriving like it was a fire sale.

The flamboyant Geraci never one to let the grass grow under his feet was telling visitors his prices were right. He barked into the phone:

"Fifteen dollars for a topless session. That's for fifteen minutes. Twenty five dollars is a session on a padded table. Thirty five dollars is for a session on a waterbed."

Vince Geraci — flamboyant massage parlor operator who had a knack for antagonizing powerful people.

Cameraman Lasker had the task of filming an actual massage. In good taste of course. With subdued lighting and shooting the masseuse and her customer in silhouette, Lasker was able to provide footage that could pass the scrutiny of any sharp-eyed censor. The piece aired on our ten P.M. and midnight casts so that kiddies wouldn't be around to ask their parents any embarrassing questions. Surprisingly the customers didn't seem concerned that they were seen inside a massage parlor. In fact, several were interviewed for the piece. The story got good viewership. The massage parlors were starting to become conversation pieces in Chicago. Soon carbon copies of Geraci's parlors began cropping up around town. They were money makers.

But it wasn't long before Geraci began rubbing people the wrong way. Community groups marched in front of The Haven, carrying placards reading "Heave the Haven." The vice squad began making almost daily forays to the parlors charging the masseuses with prostitution.

Geraci fought back. He claimed his places of business were private clubs. He staged demonstrations of his own at both a police station and City Hall. His stable of women employees carried signs stating that they were being harassed by police. One night haven masseuses staged a "lay in," at his North Wells Street store, showering Geraci and other male employees with talcum powder. It was a great stunt to generate business. Geraci also took pokes at the establishment, constantly railing about States Attorney Edward Hanrahan. Geraci alleged that Hanrahan's attempts to shut down the massage parlors were politically motivated, a charge that Hanrahan denied.

Geraci's lucrative business also caught the eye of the crime syndicate. According to Geraci two Mob figures visited his store on North Broadway one day telling him.

"We're the Outfit's representatives here and you can't do business without our okay. We're cutting in."

Geraci said he had no choice but to give the Mob a cut of the profits. Vince claimed the Mob later had their own accountant come to his store and go over the books. According to Geraci the Outfit then ordered him to give up a bigger slice of the pie. Geraci says he objected but when he did he got worked over by a "goon."

That was the last straw for Geraci. He went to see the Feds. Geraci's cooperation resulted in an indictment against a number of hoodlums. The case went to trial and Geraci testified in court against the Mobsters who allegedly had been shaking him down. Prosecutors believed Geraci was telling the truth but the jury didn't. The Mob boys were acquitted.

Defense attorneys had a field day portraying Geraci as a sleazeball who ran dirty bookstores. Granted Geraci, who always sported a sinister looking dark beard, was no pillar of society. But I've always felt he was telling the truth on the witness stand.

After his stint as a witness you may have thought that Geraci would be a target of gangland vengeance. But apparently there was never any attempt to kill him. Sheldon Davidson, who then headed the Justice Department's strike force in Chicago, told me that

FBI agents had informed certain crime syndicate figures that if anything happened to Geraci they would know where to look.

Meanwhile, the city had gotten tough with the massage parlors. They were being shut down left and right as public nuisances. Geraci, though, like the proverbial bad penny would crop up again.

Vince opened up a bathhouse on the North Side called the Geisha. He tried to circumvent the law by claiming the Geisha was strictly a place where a client could come in and unwind with a bubble bath. At the Geisha, the ads claimed "a customer could bubble his troubles away from the tip of his nose to the tip of his toes." But the police weren't impressed. Following a number of raids the bath house closed

Geraci left Chicago and moved to Alaska where reportedly for a time he ran an escort service. I was told Geraci later moved back to Chicago but if he did he has maintained a low profile which is not like him. But then again Vince might not have any other options. He rocked the boat too many times and some people have long memories.

THE SPIELER

Linn Burton probably was in more bedrooms in Chicago than the sandman. Burton's nocturnal visits were courtesy of the late show where he hawked everything under the sun from used cars to household appliances. Linn felt he could close a deal on anything and liked to describe his sales pitch as "Burton for certain."

Linn was known as one take Burton at the WGN studios where for years he did spots for Burt Weiman ford. Burton is best remembered for his long association with that Ford dealership. He moved a lot of cars for Burt Weiman.

Burton made pitches on just about everything, but used cars were his specialty.

The silvery haired Burton was a great pitchman, there was no question about that. Always well groomed and distinguished looking, he looked more like a bond salesman than a used car pitchman.

Although he claimed his style was not hard sell Burton came across awfully strong on the tube.

"I will let you be the judge," Burton would sternly intone to his TV audience. Patting a car's fender like it was his favorite grand-child, Burton would begin his pitch.

"This is an air conditioned 1977 Chevy Impala nine passenger wagon. And at this low $1,988 full delivered price, you can see that March madness has really taken over out here."

Short and sweet but effective. Burton sold cars, no doubt about it. Burton's credentials included a great voice that had a ring of sin-cerity to it.

In his heyday from the late 1950s to the early 70s Burton was the top spieler on Chicago television. Linn felt he got his gift of gab from his clergyman father.

"My dad was a Methodist minister and he was a powerful min-ister. He was good. He could save souls when nobody else could. And I think a lot of that stuff rubbed off on me. I went the other direction, though, you know."

Linn went into broadcasting during the depression. He said he beat out two hundred other applicants for an announcing job that paid a princely sum of thirty-five dollars a week. But he quickly caught on with advertisers and soon was one of the most successful free lance radio announcers in Chicago. It was only natural that after the war Burton would try his hand at television. Burton had good stage presence and that combined with his voice and style soon began opening some doors.

In television's infancy commercials were live and Burton one day fondly recalled for us some of the zany stunts he pulled to attract viewers.

"Everything was ad lib and one time I said we're going to turn the town upside down with prices. So I stood on my head and unbeknownst to me, after doing three or four minutes, all of a sud-den I started to conk out. And I fell down and when it was time to do the next commercial there was no Burton because Burton was still out."

Burton felt his familiar face reaped benefits for his clients. That, plus certain tricks of the trade gave him an edge over the average TV pitchman. Linn explained his trade secrets this way:

"It's the usage of words. I pause at odd places to emphasize certain things. Then there's the usage of the hands, people take note of these little things."

For a time Burton wore two hats, those of a restaurant operator as well as those of a television announcer. But he closed his North Side eatery in the late 1970s to concentrate on television work.

But by the time the 1980s had rolled around, the industry had changed considerably. Ad agencies wanted slick or gimmicking spots usually pre packaged on film or video tape. And some car dealers decided to get into the act themselves. They did their own commercials. Not that Burton didn't get any work but things weren't quite the same.

In some ways Linn Burton was a television pioneer. He was emulated and copied by others. Linn Burton is gone now, he died in 1995. Somehow I don't think late night TV will ever be the same. If that movie you were watching was a "dog" at least you could look forward to a Burton commercial. Yes, it was a treat to watch Burton in action. He was the consummate salesman. In fact, if Burton was around today I'd even buy a used car from him. You always believed you were getting a square deal from Linn.

THE COLLEGE OF COMPLEXES

Myron "Slim" Brundage was born in an insane asylum and died attending a senior citizens bingo party in El Centro, California. A critic of "Slim" once opined that Brundage should have never left the mental hospital where both his parents worked. "Slim" was quite a character but his free wheeling style did rub some people the wrong way.

Brundage made the most of his eighty six years working as a housepainter, a mill hand, a bartender, and an organizer for the Industrial Workers of the World, also known as the "Wobblies."

Brundage often took unpopular stands on the issues of the day. Some said "Slim" did that just to be ornery. But there was no question that Brundage's political views were way left of center. "Slim" never tried to hide the fact that he was a radical. As he told me in a 1980 interview:

"I'm a radical. I'm so far left of the communist party that they wouldn't let me in even if I wanted to get in..."

"Slim" is best known for his creation, "The College of Complexes" that for years served Chicagoans as a forum for free speech. How Brundage was able to bankroll his pet project is a story in itself. Legend has it that "Slim" fell off of an elevated platform in New York in 1951 and used the money from an insurance settlement to start the "college."

The "college" didn't grant degrees but instead was an indoor version of Chicago's "Bughouse Square" where speakers would stand on a soapbox at a near North Side park and expound their views. As time went on the park became a haven for jackrollers and male prostitutes. So the gang that loved the soapbox routine began seeking an indoor site. That's when Brundage got into the act with his "College of Complexes."

Myron "Slim" Brundage — Chicago character who founded the College of Complexes

The "students" and "faculty" would meet once a week, usually at night, at a North Side restaurant. Not all eateries were eager to play host to the "college" and it's rambunctious "students." Several locations served as the "campus" until Brundage found a permanent home at a restaurant in a run down Clark Street hotel, the St. Regis.

Tuition for each session was two dollars but that didn't include the food and beverage. The St. Regis had a full liquor license which helped insure that each gathering would be lively.

There was a guest "professor" each week and heaven forbid if he or she were thin skinned. Students would stand up and lambaste the speaker or the speaker's views. Often the speakers were heckled before they could finish their presentations and sometimes persons in the audience would begin firing verbal potshots at each other. That kind of give and take would sometimes leave the featured "professor" speechless and bewildered. Despite all the verbal salvos tempers rarely got to the point where disputes were settled with fisticuffs.

It's no wonder that the "college" would often go up for grabs. Speakers ran the gamut from nazis and beatniks to anarchists and atheists. One night while visiting the "college" with a mini cam crew, a suburban minister took an unmerciful tongue lashing from his mostly atheist audience. One "student" apparently angry over something that was said interrupted the proceedings by shouting:

"You people are nothing more than a bunch of faking and pious hypocrites. And there's an old saying if you don't like the heat get out of the kitchen."

With that the "student" stormed out of class amidst a rash of catcalls and scattered applause.

The Chicago area is home to a number of prestigious institutions of higher learning including the University of Chicago and Northwestern University. The "college of complexes" wasn't in their league. It didn't grant degrees. It didn't have any ivy covered walls. And it wasn't accredited by any reputable agency. But it was very unique just the same.

Brundage called his college a playground for people who think. He claimed he didn't try to force any agenda or curriculum on his students. As "Slim" put it:

"I never tried to save the world. That's for somebody else."

"Slim" is gone now, so is the "College of Complexes," and so too is "Bughouse square," Chicago's outdoor version of the "college." People have suggested a number of reasons why such free wheeling forums are things of the past. Some contend that a number of factors are responsible for their demise. They cite television, VCRs, the move to suburbia and exurbia, the jogging and health club craze, political correctness. You name it.

But I think one former "Bughouse Square" regular best summed up the reason for the passing of the "college" and similar forums when he said: "The whole world is Bughouse Square, now."

THE MASSEUR

Another one of our Chronicles profiled a man who had worked for over forty years as a masseur at a downtown health club.

Bill Bittner's sinewy hands had soothed thousands of aching muscles in those four decades. Bill had been a fixture at the Postl health club since 1938 and in a lifetime of helping Chicago businessmen shed excess suet Bittner had never rubbed anyone the wrong way.

Most of Bill's customers were locals but he had his share of celebrity clientele as well. Bittner rattled off the names of Bob Hope, Paul Newman, and former Teamster leader Jimmy Hoffa to name a few. He also mentioned that some of the local syndicate boys would drop in now and then for a rub down.

One of Bittner's favorites was the former heavyweight wrestling champion, Jim Londos, known as the "Golden Greek." Londos was not only a good wrestler but in his prime, was one of the world's best built men.

When Londos visited Postl's, Bittner was just getting launched in his career as a masseur so Bill, at first, was somewhat in awe of the former champ. But Bittner says that because of the rubdown he gave Londos he earned Londos' grudging respect. Bittner says that Londos tested him when he came to the rubdown table: "He wanted a hard massage, so when he asked for a hard massage, I gave it to him. And he says, 'Kid, I like it deep but not that hard.' so I smile to myself. I improvise, I use my forearms and my elbows. He was grunting and I was giving it to him. I smiled, and after that he became my friend."

Bittner was sixty five years old when we interviewed him. His hair was still coal black and although his biceps were starting to lose some definition, Bill was still put together very well.

In his heyday at Postl's, Bittner and his fellow masseurs gave around one hundred and seventy five massages a day. But by 1979 Bill was the only masseur still working at the health club. He was doing about five massages a day. So Bittner had other duties at the club including the laundry detail. Some masseurs would have complained that such duties were beneath them. But Bill was no prima donna. Besides he needed the job.

Bittner never made big money and at one time was so strapped for a buck that he hardly had enough cash to pay for a marriage license. It must have been true love since Bill and the Mrs. weren't able to afford a honeymoon or even a reception. But Bill said he and his better half just had to grin and bear it: "It cost me three dollars for the license, five bucks for the judge to marry us. So I took the wife to the tavern. We had a stein of beer apiece and she went home and I went to work."

Bittner, a graduate of the National College of Swedish Massage, at one time flirted with the idea of finding fame and fortune in the prize ring. But in looking back, Bittner felt he put his dukes to better use.

Bill, though was almost kayoed by "John Barleycorn." At one point, Bittner said, his drinking got so bad that he became concerned that his clients might get the idea that the fumes around them weren't coming from rubbing alcohol. So Bittner, after the urging of some of his friends, quit cold turkey and went on the wagon. He told me that he hadn't a drop of liquor in years.

Postl's which was a throwback to another era isn't around anymore. It couldn't compete with the new breed of health clubs that have been cropping up in recent years. Aerobics, stairmasters, nautilus machines, juice bars, and all the trimmings are geared to busy young professionals of both sexes. Somehow it wouldn't seem right to go to the Postl health club to see if you could get a date for that night.

But that was then and this is now.

TIGER JOE

Joseph Marusich came back to his Chicago roots in 1985 after a lengthy sojourn in California. The name Joseph Marusich probably doesn't ring a bell because Marusich was better known by his nom de guerre of Tiger Joe Marsh, a professional wrestler and actor.

Tiger Joe Marsh wasn't exactly a household word either but the odds are readers of this epic saw Marsh toiling as a villain in the movies or on their favorite TV show. Tiger Joe played a bad guy in such Hollywood blockbusters as "On the Waterfront," "Panic in the Streets," "Viva Zapata," and "From Russia with Love," to name just a few. You could also spot Tiger Joe's bald head and constant scowl on numerous TV shows, most always in the role of a villain. Marsh was six feet tall and weighed two hundred and sixty pounds, so the theatergoer didn't need much of an imagination to picture Tiger Joe as a fearsome thug.

Marsh served his thespian apprenticeship on the pro mat circuit where he grappled long enough to become a claimant for the world's heavyweight championship. That was back in 1937. In those days the mat game had less burlesque to it than is the case today. Joe's elaborate tiger striped robe was his trademark when he entered the squared circle to do battle. He got into wrestling as a young man learning his trade in the Bridgeport neighborhood of Chicago. Soon he was a headliner grappling in such Chicago arenas as Rainbow Gardens and White City.

Joe said as a youth he palled around with a crew of wild kids who had their sights set on a career in the underworld. In fact, Marsh claims that future Mob boss Sam Giancana once tried to convince him to join the notorious Forty Two Gang. But Marsh said he rejected the offer because he wanted to try his hand in the ring. Tiger said he explained to the Giancana crew that he had his sights set on grappling glory:

"I told those boys that I'm not interested in making a soft living. I've got nothing against money but I'm going to become a wrestler."

Ex-pro wrestler and actor Tiger Joe Marsh relaxes in his Bridgeport home. Marsh always played the villain on the silver screen.

Tiger Joe said the Giancana crew respected his decision and never gave him a hard time about it.

Marsh was always the bad guy and never the "babyface" in his wrestling days. According to Tiger Joe he became a ring heavy because of economic considerations:

"The people always remember a villain. The good guys go hungry, the villains make the money."

In the 1950s Tiger Joe went the Hollywood route. That came about after famed director Elia Kazan asked him if he would be interested in acting in motion pictures. Marsh was no novice when Kazan approached him. He had just completed a two year stint on stage with the national company of "The Teahouse of the August Moon."

Although Marsh was most always a heavy on the silver screen, there were a few exceptions. Larry Hagman of Dallas fame once directed Joe in an epic called "Beware of the Blob." In that film Tiger Joe was a victim and not a villain. Once when we did a profile piece on Tiger Joe we included a scene from "Beware of the Blob." In the clip we showed on the air Marsh was trapped in his bathtub by the Blob. Joe was playing the part of a man doomed by the Blob. Marsh began shouting in Croatian as the Blob came closer and closer to the bathtub. That fifteen second clip was the only scene from the movie that we used on the air. But it was enough to trigger several phone calls from irate viewers. It turned out that Tiger Joe had blasphemed God as he hollered in Croatian. From that time on, we always touched base with one of our Channel Two technicians, Diane Vrlich when Tiger Joe was on the tube. Diane is of Croatian extraction and knows the language. We didn't want any repeats of the Blob incident.

As time went on Marsh found out that parts, even small roles were getting more difficult to land. The motion picture industry had changed considerably since the day when Joe first showed up at Hollywood and Vine. Many of the producers and directors who were pals of Tiger Joe's had left the scene. For Tiger Joe the changes in the industry weren't for the better. An embittered Marsh told me, in an interview, shortly before he died:

"They lost the color, the identification. Back in the old days you knew every character, today they all look the same."

Partly at the urging of his younger brother, Anthony, Tiger Joe moved back to Chicago. Marsh was never one to let the grass grow under his feet. It wasn't long after he established residence in Bridgeport that Tiger Joe announced he was going to be involved in running a new nightclub. The new club, Joe said, would feature big bands that would play popular dance tunes of the 1930s and 40s. The nightclub was going to be called "The Tiger's Den."

But the project never really got off the ground. Tiger Joe became ill and checked himself into a hospital. He never came out. In May of 1989 Tiger Joe Marsh passed away. He was seventy-seven years old.

THE STRIPPER

These are trying days for aficionados of burlesque. There are very few, if any, palaces of peel still operating in this country. True, there are many night clubs, sometimes called gentlemen's clubs that offer exotic dancing. And there are a few theaters that feature nude dancing sandwiched in between porno movies.

But the old burlesque house with big name strippers, a live band, a chorus line, and vendors hawking cracker jacks and "French post cards" is no more.

In the 1940s and 50s strippers such as Lily St. Cyr, Georgia Southern, and Tempest Storm commanded big bucks. Those veterans were stars in their own right. They often played to full houses when they troded the boards in big city burlesque houses.

When I decided to include a stripper in our "Chicago Chronicle" series, I wanted to do a story on a relative unknown. After all the Chronicle series was geared to people who were not famous. So we came across a young woman called Athena who was the featured performer at the Oak Theater on Chicago's Northwest Side.

It turned out that Athena, billed as "Miss Nude Greece" was one of the more popular attractions that the Oak Theater had had in recent years. It also turned out that Athena wasn't from Greece but was a Hoosier from Morrisville, Indiana. And there was something else that the lotharios sitting in the front rows didn't know. Athena was always accompanied to the theater by her husband, Garvey.

Athena got her start in show business as a country and western singer. But one evening in an Indianapolis night club the featured stripper failed to show up. That gave Athena a chance to strut her stuff. Management liked her style. From then on it was good bye guitar and cowboy hat, and hello g-string and pasties.

Athena — "Miss Nude Greece" — was actually a Hoosier who hailed from Morrisville, Indiana.

By burlesque standards Athena was diminutive and less busty than most of her contemporaries. Although Athena may have been less endowed physically than some of her rivals she didn't have to take a back seat to anyone. Her sensuous dance kept the audience riveted to its seats.

When we interviewed Athena, she had been an exotic dancer for only six years, not a veteran by burlesque standards. But she had served her apprenticeship well. She had patterned her style after two of the burlesque immortals we mentioned earlier, Lily St. Cyr and Tempest Storm.

Athena was willing to share with our viewers some of the tricks of the trade. As she explained it: "the slower you take your clothes off, it leaves more to the imagination. Your gimmick is your body, it's like the flowing, the slowness. And as you remove your costume, it should be done with class and finesse…You take a girl who just takes her clothes off or throws it here and there. It takes away the tenderness a woman is supposed to portray."

Athena preferred working theaters rather than playing the night club circuit because as she put it: "There's less hassle with drunks at a theater."

Athena contended that the theater crowd was more passive and laid back. Stage door Johnnies weren't a problem, according to

Athena, since hubby Garvey was a constant companion.

On the subject of wedded bliss, Athena claimed it just came naturally for a stripper. Athena went into a long discourse on how to hang on to your man:

"The women who are strippers have a different attitude than your little housewife. I'm not knocking housewives, God forbid, because I am one. What I'm saying is, you've heard the old saying that you find a girl who is a hooker or a stripper or a girl of the night, if she ever settles down and gets married, she makes the best wife in the whole world. We understand the male generation. It's interesting to sit in the lobby of the theater and count the wedding bands that come through the door. In my book, if things were right at home, they wouldn't be here."

Athena described herself as a country girl at heart. But said she had no intention of hanging up her g-string in the near future. Athena claimed that when she retired from show business she'd find happiness working at her hubby's bodyshop down in little Morrisville, Indiana.

One final note before we close this episode on the bump and grind circuit. The shills at the old burlesque houses used to tout the midnight show as a "katy bar the door performance." Those midnight shows were supposed to be no holds barred sessions where the strippers would take everything off and gyrate wildly on the stage.

But Tempest Storm once told me the facts of burlesque house life. "Honey," she said, "the best show takes place in the morning or early afternoon. That's when the girls are the freshest. By midnight, our tails are dragging, we just want to get done and go home."

If Tempest was right, and she ought to know, the kiddie matinee wasn't only the best show but the cheapest, too. Ticket prices for the morning and early afternoon performances, were as a rule, a lot less than the evening shows.

And there was another drawback for the night owls. The vendors' supply of those naughty postcards, that we told you about earlier was more often than not, sold out by the time the midnight show was getting underway.

JELLY HOLT

Lindsley "Jelly" Holt personified what our "Chicago Chronicle" series was all about. He wasn't a headliner but a decent hard working Chicagoan who had an interesting story to tell.

"Jelly" was working for the city's Department of Streets and Sanitation when we ran across him back in 1980. Holt, a back man, had grown up on Chicago's South Side or "Bronzeville" as it was known when "Jelly" was a youngster.

When we profiled Holt, he was sixty six years old and had a desk job at the department's City Hall headquarters. His task was to handle complaints from residents who were unhappy with their garbage pick up or other Street and San. functions. However, "Jelly's" experiences as a bureaucrat weren't the focus of our story.

You see, Lindsley "Jelly" Holt was really at home when he was perched behind a set of skins, drumming out one of his favorite numbers. "Jelly," who was on the rotund side, had a life long love affair with drums, having acquired his first set while still in grade school.

For twenty seven years Holt had his own combo, "The Blazes," which played all over the city. Lindsley's group entertained at South Side "black and tans" as well as plush loop cocktail lounges.

The nickname, "Jelly," stemmed from a moniker Holt's school chums pinned on him when he was an aspiring cager in grade school.

"I used to play basketball and I had a peculiar way of bouncing the ball. I'd bounce it up and down like a bowl of jelly going from side to side. Then, later on, I started playing drums and I had a habit. I'd get happy, I'd bounce up and down, so they named me "Jelly" and it stuck with me ever since."

Lindsley "Jelly" Holt said John Dillinger gave him money for a new set of drums.

Holt vividly recalled his days as a fledgling musician when getting good club dates for black artists was next to impossible. Lindsley apparently played in some tough joints in that period. He claims he once had his drums riddled by a shot gun wielding hoodlum by the name of "Three Fingers" Jack White. But Holt claimed he came out of that harrowing experience with a new set of drums, thanks to, of all people, John Dillinger.

But let's have "Jelly" explain the incident in his own words. Holt said that White, who had been drinking heavily, approached him during a break and said:

'Boy, how much do them drums cost?'

Holt: "'I paid 35 dollars for them.' He says, 'is that all?' He says, 'get out of them I want to hear a loud bang.' He immediately took a shot gun and blowed them drums all to pieces and I took to crying. And then the one they called John Dillinger came up. I will never forget it. He looked at me with those gray eyes, you know. I'll never forget that look and he said 'Don't worry about the drums, I'll take care of it.' He had money. I never saw so much money. There were a lot of one hundred dollar bills. And he peeled off five bills and said to a guy they called Doc, 'Buy him some drums.'"

So "Jelly" got a new set of drums all because of the generosity of a man Holt claimed was John Dillinger.

Holt was more than just a drummer. He was also a vocalist and arranger. And one number "My Hat's on the Side of My Head" came out on a United label in the early 1950s.

Television, the demise of many night clubs, and changing tastes in music left Holt little option but to disband his combo in 1962.

Oh, he still played a few dates but it wasn't like the old days. "Jelly" said he would have really gotten into the dumps if it wasn't for his wife Catherine. Holt said his better half kept his spirits up during some tough times. Catherine even urged "Jelly" to give tin pan alley one more shot. But times had changed and Holt was content to pick up a steady pay check from the city.

No, you never read about Lindsley "Jelly" Holt in the Chicago guide books or travel brochures but, he hit high C in one of our Chicago Chronicles.

IWO JIMA HERO

Joseph Jeremiah McCarthy was thirty three, the oldest man in his company, when he hit the beach on a tiny island in the Pacific called Iwo Jima. It was February of 1945 and the war with Japan was at it's height, when McCarthy, a Marine Captain, landed at Iwo Jima, an eight mile chunk of rock and ash. McCarthy was Commanding Officer of George Company, Second Battalion, 24th Regiment of the Fourth Marine Division.

McCarthy, a South Sider, had been an outstanding athlete at Chicago's Englewood High School where he starred on the football and baseball teams. The husky McCarthy, a six footer, joined the fire department in 1940 and served at a South Side truck company until he entered the service. McCarthy always kept himself in tip top shape and the Marines were right up Joe's alley. McCarthy's passion for physical conditioning may have been a factor as to how he survived the war. He dodged his share of enemy bullets but as McCarthy explained: "I could run like a deer."

McCarthy in 1945 was no neophyte when it came to leading his men into combat. Before Iwo he made landings at Saipan and Tinian, two other dots on a map that the Japanese had defended fiercely. At Saipan McCarthy was awarded the Silver Star for carrying two wounded Marines to safety.

Although Saipan was a rough go it was only a preliminary bout to the savage fighting that lay ahead at Iwo. Iwo may not have been a pretty piece of real estate but it was important from a strategic standpoint. The island was near Japan proper, only six hundred air miles from Tokyo. If U.S. Forces could take Iwo Jima, B-29's from the Strategic Air Command would be three hours closer to targets in the Japanese homeland. It would also enable the bombers to have fighter escorts on their runs, something that wasn't feasible from far away bases at Saipan and Tinian.

The Marines were led to believe that a massive bombardment by the Navy had softened up Iwo's defenses. But McCarthy felt the Marines were in for a long and tough fight. His sense of foreboding proved correct. The first and second waves landed with little or no resistance. But the Japanese were playing possum.

When McCarthy and his men hit the beach as part of the third wave, all hell broke loose. The enemy opened up. McCarthy and his company realized Iwo was not going to be any cakewalk. McCarthy looked at the scene around him: "The beach was loaded with equipment, dead Marines, dead Navy medics and dead sailors from the landing barges."

I did lengthy interviews with McCarthy on several occasions. In one instance I spent almost a day at Joe's summer home in northern Wisconsin. He was in an expansive mood that time, perhaps because the 40th anniversary of V-J day was nearing. But it was obvious that it pained McCarthy to discuss the heavy casualties that the men under his command had suffered: "I landed on Iwo with two hundred and fifty four men and seven officers. By the time I was wounded there were only twelve men left in my company."

McCarthy was wounded leading his men up Hill 382, a chunk of real estate that McCarthy's superiors felt had strategic value. So Joe, along with a flamethrower team and a rifle squad went over the top. McCarthy and his men dashed seventy five yards under heavy enemy fire. While Japanese gunners, concealed in pillboxes, raked the Marines mercilessly McCarthy's crew wasn't idle. Flamethrowers, BAR's, and grenades, some thrown by McCarthy did their gruesome work. Three pillboxes were knocked out of action.

McCarthy was seriously injured by enemy mortar fire. But the Marines had taken Hill 382, a turning point in a fierce and bloody battle. For McCarthy, the war was over. He went stateside where his wounds were treated at a naval hospital.

Joe McCarthy, awarded the Medal of Honor by President Truman.

McCarthy's actions on Iwo did not go unnoticed. For gallantry above and beyond the call of duty Captain McCarthy was awarded the nation's highest military decoration, the Medal of Honor.

In ceremonies in Washington, in October of 1945, President Harry Truman placed the prestigious ribbon around the marine hero's neck. It was a moment McCarthy said he would never forget. "After he presented the medal to me I shook hands with him and President Truman said to me 'Captain McCarthy I'd rather have that medal than be President of the United States.'"

McCarthy survived Iwo Jima but a lot of his comrades did not. In the thirty five day campaign U.S. casualties numbered twenty six thousand, including six thousand dead. For the Japanese the death toll was even higher. Of the island's twenty thousand defenders, only one thousand survived.

Although McCarthy remained in the reserves he rejoined the fire department and became the supervisor of the department's ambulance service. Joe attacked problems surrounding his new job with the same zeal he had with the Marines. He was instrumental in modernizing the ambulance service and also pushed hard to increase the number of ambulances in the Department's inventory. When McCarthy took over the ambulance service in 1946, there were only four ambulances. When McCarthy retired in 1973 the department had thirty six.

McCarthy left Chicago after his fire department days. Joe and his second wife Jean spent the summers at their home in Phelps, Wisconsin and when the leaves began to fall the McCarthys would head to their condo at Delray beach, Florida. Retirement was kind to McCarthy but he always made it a point to show up for reunions with his old Marine Corps buddies.

Joe lived long enough to attend ceremonies marking the 50th anniversary of the Iwo Jima battle. He was honored, along with other veterans of the island bloodbath, in ceremonies presided over by President Clinton. And McCarthy returned to his old stompin' ground the same month for an affair at the Chicago Hilton and Towers. McCarthy, by that time was the only surviving Chicago World War II Medal of Honor winner.

In June of 1996, the man known as "Chicago's Fighting Fireman" died in Delray beach, Florida. Joe was eighty three when he succumbed. We did our last interview with McCarthy in February of 1995 when he was in Chicago for the Iwo ceremonies at the Hilton. I asked him why, at his age, would he be gallivanting around the country for so many reunions? Joe replied, "My boys want to see me, and I want to see these men and they are real men who have done so much for their country. I can't let them down."

CHAPTER FIVE

They Took the Stand

TOKYO JOE

Ken Eto was one of few persons in Chicago to have ever been taken for a "ride" and live to tell about it.

Eto who was known in underworld circles as "Tokyo Joe," "Joe Montana," or "Joe the Jap" was actually of Korean extraction and not Japanese. Whatever moniker you give Eto he will go down in Chicago Mob lore as a guy who took three slugs at close range and survived, none the worse for wear.

Eto's brush with death occurred on February 10, 1983 when an Outfit assassin fired three shots into Eto's skull. Ken survived because he had a thick skull, was a good actor, and was lucky.

For years Eto had headed the Chicago crime syndicate's gambling operations in the Hispanic community. But in early 1983 Eto was facing a prison term after being convicted on Federal gambling charges. Eto's Mob superiors apparently felt Ken would spill the beans to the Feds rather than go to prison. Despite Eto's reputation as a standup guy Ken's bosses felt they couldn't take a chance. They opted to have Eto hit.

Eto, in an interview with Federal authorities after the assassination attempt insisted he had no intention of informing on his Mob colleagues. It was only after the aborted hit, Eto says, that he decided to cooperate with the government.

"Tokyo Joe" claimed he smelled a rat when he accepted a ride with two Mob soldiers, Jasper Campise and John Gattuso. According to Eto the two men were to take him to a dinner meeting with Vince Solano, one of Ken's bosses.

Ken Eto, AKA "Tokyo Joe," (author on right) leaves the Criminal Courts Building. Eto was "taken for a ride" and lived to tell about it.

Eto, interviewed by Federal authorities, hours after he had been shot, told an incredible story. Egged on by his interrogators, Ken described how he had faked his own death. And then Eto made his decision to trade in his black hat for a white one. He opted to go into the Federal witness protection program.

He told FBI agent William Brown, assistant U.S. Attorney Jeremy Margolis, and Chicago Police detectives how he met Campise and Gattuso in the parking lot of a Northwest Side American Legion Hall. The assailants suggested Eto use his car. "Johnny sat in the back, Jay sat in the front….Jay is talking about this little Italian place, it's so nice and good you know."

Eto drove to Grand and Harlem where Campise directed him to pull into a parking lot. Solano allegedly was to meet Eto there. "Pull back by some railroad tracks," Campise told Eto. It was then that Eto says Gattuso shot him in the head three times. "When they shot, I could hear a bang, cluck, bang, cluck, maybe three or four times."

The resourceful Eto pretended he had been fatally shot: "so I started shaking like make believe that I'm finished. And I'm on the seat but I hear bang, bang, I mean ,uh, the doors close, that means they're taking off."

After Eto felt his would be killers had fled the scene he got out of the car and walked to a nearby drug store. There Eto asked the store owner Murray Robinson for help. Robinson promptly called a police dispatcher who didn't seem to realize the gravity of Eto's condition. A partial transcript of the phone conversation follows:

Robinson: "This is Terminal Pharmacy at 7029 West Grand."

Dispatcher: "Yeah."

Robinson: "I just had a man come in here whose real bloody, he's all covered with blood and says he's been shot. Can you send a, a, an officer and a, uh ambulance?"

Dispatcher: "Where's he at now?"

Robinson: "He's right here in the store."

Dispatcher: "Put him on the phone."

Robinson: "Well, he's quite a mess, hold on one second."

Dispatcher: "What's your problem sir?"

Finally, after what seemed to be marathon negotiations an ambulance was sent and Eto was rushed to the hospital.

Detectives who investigated the botched hit believe Ken was saved because of a faulty silencer on the twenty two caliber gun. Investigators felt the faulty silencer reduced the muzzle velocity of the bullets. Another theory is that the would be killers used faulty ammunition. At any rate Eto lived to tell his incredible story. And tell it he did. Eto appeared as a government witness in a number of Mob trials.

On one occasion Eto, garbed in a black robe, testified before a Presidential commission that was investigating organized crime. Ken's face was fully covered, and his Outfit resembled a Ku Klux Klan costume except it was black rather than white. The media loved the sartorial gimmick and Eto's testimony received heavy electronic and print coverage.

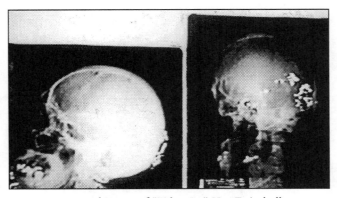

Hospital X-rays of "Tokyo Joe" Ken Eto's skull
after he survived a Mob hit.

Eto's would-be assassins were not forgotten either. Despite warnings by prosecutors that they faced gangland retribution for their incompetence. Both Jasper Campise and John Gattuso shrugged off warnings of dire peril and posted bond. The two men had been offered protective custody but they turned it down. Campise reportedly had told friends that since he had been a "loyal soldier" and was close to several Mob higher ups no harm would come to him.

The case never came to trial. In fact it was settled out of court in a very grim way. In July, of 1983, five months after the attempt on Eto's life, the bodies of Campise and Gattuso were found stuffed in the trunk of a car. Both men had been stabbed repeatedly.

Mob experts said the murders of the two men were warnings to other soldiers to "cut the mustard" or face the consequences. No one has ever been charged in the slayings of Campise and Gattuso.

The reader may wonder as to what happened to Ken Eto. Other than periodic court appearances as a government witness, Eto hasn't been spotted in the Chicago area for some time. One day we ran into a pal of Ken's, a Chicago cab driver by the name of Raymond Tom. Tom opined that Eto was living the good life, possibly in Brazil. If Eto is spending his days in Latin America the Feds aren't saying. After all "Tokyo Joe" still has a few enemies around. It wouldn't be a bright idea to say where he hangs his hat, would it?

THE INFORMANT

For seventeen years William "Red" Wemette led a double life. To the Chicago Mob he was a peddler of pornography, vulnerable to extortion. But to the FBI he was a valuable informant on the Chicago Outfit. Wemette played a high stakes game. If the Mob found out that he was working the other side of the street it would have been curtains for the former Marine.

Wemette let the FBI install a concealed video camera in his Old Town apartment. For a fifteen month period the camera recorded "Red" meeting and paying off organized crime figures who were shaking him down, a practice known as a street tax.

Wemette realized he was playing with dynamite, a slip up could be fatal. He told me shortly after his testimony sent two Mobsters to prison:" I considered it dangerous. I was told that from the first day. I'd of definitely been murdered, there's no doubt in my mind."

"Red" was in the pornography business for some fifteen years. He sold sexually explicit books and movies from his Wells Street store that was located in what is known as the Old Town neighborhood in Chicago. Wemette's introduction to the crime syndicate came well before his book store days. "Red" told me that he tended bar for a while in a lounge owned by the Mob. In that role he met a number of Mob underlings. Wemette was able to see first hand how the Chicago Outfit did business. He says he didn't like what he saw: "I saw these people literally getting away with murder. They were bullies and they took advantage of people that couldn't defend themselves and nobody wanted to come forward."

Wemette says he sought out the FBI, offering to become a government mole. His first meeting with the Feds took place, not at a fancy restaurant or plush hotel, but in the Lion House of the Lincoln Park Zoo. Wemette says, unlike most other would be informants, he was not in trouble with "Uncle Sam," and was not the target of any criminal investigation or grand jury probe. Wemette claims his motive for cooperation was not financial gain or notoriety. "Red" contends his motivation for undertaking such a dangerous assignment was because of his hatred of organized crime and what it stood for.

"Red" concedes he was paid for information. He says he got about ten thousand dollars from the FBI for his cooperation. But Wemette considers the ten grand a paltry amount in exchange for leading a double life.

In 1974 Wemette opened his Old Town book store, then called "The Peeping Tom." Business apparently was good from the beginning of the venture. The Mob soon took notice. It was the kind of operation that the Outfit loved to muscle in on. In the 1970s owners of adult book stores and gay bars were often preyed upon by the crime syndicate. The Mob found such businesses susceptible to shake downs. Soon Wemette was forking over two hundred and fifty dollars a week as a street tax. Wemette said his Mob collectors later established a monthly payment of eleven hundred dollars that was described by his underworld associates as "a nice round figure."

By 1987 Wemette and the Feds decided to try and hit pay dirt. It was then that the video camera was installed in "Red's" second floor apartment above the book store. The combination of the camera, complete with sound, and Wemette's testimony in Federal court convinced a jury to convict two men on attempted extortion charges. The trial was Wemette's baptism of fire on the witness stand. He withstood a blistering cross examination by one of Chicago's better criminal lawyers Allan Ackerman. Prosecutors were ecstatic about Red's performance. He was credible and then some.

One of the two men convicted was Frank "The German" Schweihs, who Federal authorities had labeled as a feared Mob enforcer and a suspect in a number of gangland murders. The jury, court buffs, and the media got an earful from the video tapes as Schweihs was heard boasting about his past exploits. It was an inside look at how a long time Mob strongman talked and acted.

In one of the taped conversations, Schweihs went into a lengthy discourse of how he had the authority and the power to protect Wemette from other organized crime figures who might want a piece of "Red's" business. With the videotape rolling Schweihs was heard to say: "This fuckin' joint (Wemette's book store) has been declared for years. There's no one has the right to come in and fuck in our domain. I don't give a fuck, who the fuck it is, if it's Al Capone's brother and he comes back, okay. This is a declared joint, and no one has the right to come and fuck with this, okay!"

Government videotape reveals William "Red" Wemette paying off Mob enforcer Frank Schweihs in Wemette's apartment. Justice Department photo.

"Red" and his partner, Lenny Cross had a couple of close calls with the unsuspecting Schweihs. On one occasion when the "German" had stopped at the apartment for a payment, Wemette said, Frank inadvertently pulled two cushions forward, exposing two concealed microphones. "Red" said he quickly called Schweihs' attention to a fancy lighter he had placed on the table. While Frank closely examined the lighter Wemette rearranged the cushions so that the microphones could no longer be seen.

Wemette had no delusions about who he was dealing with. "Red" was playing with fire. As Wemette told me after the Schweihs trial: "he was probably one of the most ruthless, aggressive individuals in the Chicago Mob that I ever met. The most dangerous."

In February of 1990 Schweihs, then fifty nine years old, was sentenced to thirteen years in prison. Now Schweihs and his confederate were never charged with extortion itself. That's because Wemette was a paid informant at the time of the shakedowns. The money that Wemette was handing over to the Mob was not actually Wemette's but the Federal Governments.

Following the trial Wemette dropped from sight. At the age of forty he was starting life all over again. He was given a new name, new identification, and even a new birth certificate. After Schweihs had been sentenced we interviewed Wemette at a site far away from Chicago. The one time book store owner was an embittered man. He claimed the FBI had let him down. He said the Feds were dragging their feet over some money that was owed him. He eventually got his money. According to Wemette that didn't happen until he had filed a lawsuit. An angry Wemette contended that once his usefulness was over, he was dropped by the Justice Department like a hot potato. The government denied treating "Red" shabbily but Wemette wouldn't buy that.

Constantly on Wemette's mind was the fear that the Mob would seek retribution. against him. As he put it: "I will always look over my shoulder, I'll always look behind my back."

When I interviewed Wemette in early 1990 I figured that was the last we would hear about him as newsmaker. But I was wrong. "Red" soon resurfaced, again in the role of a key government witness.

In September of 1995 a southwest suburban stable owner, Kenneth Hansen, went on trial for the murder of three young boys. A murder that had occurred forty years earlier. The 1955 slayings of Robert Peterson and brothers John and Anton Schuessler had been one of the most sensational homicides in Chicago history. The slayings had baffled investigators for years. The case appeared unsolvable until 1994 when detectives and prosecutors put a full court press on the investigation. Men who had known Hansen for years came forward with new information. That plus solid police work led to Hansen's indictment and ultimate conviction.

One of those who played a key role in the Hansen case was Wemette. "Red" had prodded lawmen for some time that he believed he knew the identity of the Schuessler-Peterson killer. Wemette had become familiar with Hansen in 1968 shortly after Wemette had gotten out of the Marine Corps. "Red," then nineteen years old, told investigators that he had been seduced by Hansen who had a record of sexually abusing young men and boys.

"Red's" insistence that lawmen could nail Hansen on the triple murder intrigued investigators. Wemette told detectives that while he and Hansen once sipped scotch whiskey, the stable owner confided in him and told him about a very famous case. According to Wemette, Hansen said he picked up three boys who were hitchhiking and took them to a Northwest Side stable where he sexually abused them. Wemette said that Hansen admitted killing two of the boys and said his late brother, Curt Hansen killed the third youngster.

That was basically the same story that Wemette told a criminal court jury. Wemette was one of several prosecution witnesses who implicated Hansen in the triple slaying.

But "Red" had the largest entourage of bodyguards at the trial. And it was Wemette who was escorted to and from the Criminal Courts building like a potentate. Federal authorities were fearful that Mobsters with long memories would seek revenge against the former book store owner. The heavy security made it obvious that the government planned to get more mileage out of Wemette in other criminal investigations.

As for Hansen, it took the jury less than two hours to find him guilty of the triple slaying. Hansen who was sixty two at the time of the 1995 trial was sentenced to life in prison.

"Red" has moved several times since the Hansen trial. Authorities want Wemette to keep at least one step ahead of any potential assassins. Wemette has been working hand in hand with the ATF, looking into several unsolved murders. "Red" reportedly has information on several very old criminal cases. Information that could be critical in gaining an indictment.

Wemette was not a happy camper after the Schweihs trial ended. But now "Red" and the Feds have kissed and made up. Wemette has nothing but praise for his latest "handler," John Rotunno of the Treasury Department. "Red" calls Rotunno the "best government agent I ever worked with in my life."

So Chicago hasn't seen the last of William "Red" Wemette. Don't be surprised if Wemette pops up in the witness box in some future high profile trial. But don't rule out Wemette as a major player even if he doesn't testify. Wemette moved in some rugged circles for a time. He has an excellent memory and often is able to come up with some juicy tid bits that can help jump start an investigation into an old case that has long been forgotten.

CHAPTER SIX

The Distaff Side

LADIES OF THE NIGHT

In early 1978 we made a pilgrimage to Las Vegas to do a story on the late Tony Spilotro, a transplanted Chicagoan, who was then making a name for himself in the gambling Mecca. Spilotro, a feared enforcer, had been sent out west to look after the Chicago Mob's interests in Las Vegas.

The brass at WBBM-TV though, wanted to get more mileage out of our trip. They suggested we do a two part series on Spilotro and his cohorts but also write a couple of pieces about Vegas, a favorite haunt of many Chicago area residents. The regime's reasoning made sense. Other than the Los Angeles and Phoenix markets Chicago sends more visitors to Las Vegas than any other city. Stories about Vegas, as a general rule, do well on Chicago television.

The series on Spilotro was both an artistic and ratings success. But a subsequent story about the Vegas scene did even better. We reported on the numerous wedding chapels, the schools for dealers, the sports books, the prime rib wars, the battle for convention dollars between Las Vegas and Chicago, and the impact of Atlantic City on the Nevada casinos. All worth reporting and of interest to many of our viewers. But it was something else that turned out to be a box office bonanza.

We interviewed two high priced call girls who plied their trade in cocktail lounges along the strip. They were not common street walkers, but in the parlance of the business "high class hookers."

What made the interview unique at the time was that the two women went on camera showing their faces. Not the usual silhouette routine where the subject's face is concealed and his or her voice is distorted.

The station's promotion department got into the act and placed a large ad in two Chicago newspapers. The ad pictured two sleazy looking women sitting on bar stools. The women were local models and not our Vegas ladies. The newspaper spot got it's point across and as the saying goes sex sells. It sure does. I was told later that from the numbers standpoint we hit the jackpot, the night we ran the call girl interviews. The story had no social redeeming value but remember folks, everything is fair in love, war, and the ratings game.

Market research also revealed that more women viewers than usual caught the ten o'clock news that night. A lot of men go to Las Vegas on business or gambling junkets, often leaving the wife or girlfriend back home. Perhaps those on the distaff side wanted to see what the competition was like.

Our interview subjects, Toni and Marilyn, were two winsome working girls who didn't beat around the bush. Toni, an auburn haired beauty with a svelte figure apparently did all right in the world's oldest profession. She was candid when she described an evening on the town: "on a good night you can make four or five bills (four or five hundred dollars) when you don't have to hide from vice all night and you don't get all those jerk offs that don't want to do nothing, but sit and take up your time and be seen with a pretty girl."

Toni's reference to four or five bills a night would have been a healthy paycheck. Those were 1978 prices she was talking about.

Marilyn, a buxom brunette lass from Indiana, scoffed at the amateur competition that would come to Vegas from L.A. and Phoenix on the weekends. According to Marilyn, the amateurs, as she called them, were mostly secretaries or waitresses who would offer their services at bargain basement prices. Marilyn assured us that the amateurs didn't know how to satisfy the customers as she and Toni did. As Marilyn discreetly put it:

"For the price we charge we want distinguished clientele."

Toni had a parting word for anxious wives concerned that their mates would catch some horrible disease: "We almost guarantee that they won't take anything home to their wives."

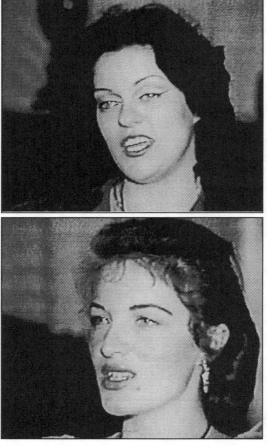

Las Vegas hookers Marilyn (top) and Toni (bottom).

Confidentially we received a number of calls from male viewers who wanted to know how they could contact Toni or Marilyn. I told these would-be lotharios that we ran into the pair at a bar in the Sands Hotel. But, I pointed out that the pair usually made the rounds at about all the better hotels on the Vegas strip.

One postscript to the Vegas story that made the bean counters at the station really happy. My camera crew told me if I could get Toni and Marilyn to go on the tube and do an interview without concealing their faces, they would not charge WBBM any overtime and would shoot the interview "on the house." And that's what happened. As they say, everybody wants their picture taken.

In Chicago most working girls looking for the carriage trade don't hang out in bars. Instead they operate through various escort services that police say are merely fronts for prostitution.

The Kay Jarrett escort service was probably the most successful and well known of the services. Kay's heyday was in the 40s and 50s although she continued to have a stable of young women in the early 1960s. Jarrett claimed she was a legitimate businesswoman who provided lonely men, in town for a convention, with dates. Kay argued that her escorts were good dancers, lively conversationalists, and nothing more.

Vice detectives, posing as conventioneers, however, had a different opinion of Kay's escorts. They would testify in court that Kay's girls would proposition them in hotel rooms and then begin to disrobe.

Kay Jarrett soon became a legend in Chicago. She had her name and phone number printed in match books. That way conventioneers seeking action didn't have to look through the yellow pages. Through an intermediary, we tried to convince Kay to do a television interview but Kay politely declined. Although Kay has long since retired she left a legacy that others have tried to fill.

When we did a series on the escort services in the late 1980s we found that they were alive and well despite the scare over AIDS. Some things just never change. Well heeled conventioneers armed with expense money to burn are the biggest source of income for the escort services.

But the cost of companionship had soared dramatically. For our 1987 series on escort services we interviewed two working girls who we called Sue and Trish. Sue told us that prices ranged from one hundred and fifty dollars an hour to five hundred dollars an hour depending on the type of service the client requested. Trish, however, pointed out that there were discounts for all night liaisons.

Many escort services, fearful that a potential customer may be an undercover police officer, posing as a businessman, are usually very cagey on the phone. Yet a Channel Two news assignment editor, Ed Marshall, had little trouble lining up a "date" by pretending to be a lonely visitor seeking fun and games. It was all in the line of duty for Marshall who was not given the opportunity to complete his undercover assignment.

Police and prostitution rings continually play a cat and mouse game. So, some of the escort services, leery of law enforcement efforts deal only with regular or former customers. Others demand to see airline tickets, credit cards, and other forms of identification to make sure the client is what he purports to be. But, despite such precautions most of the escort services eventually run afoul of the law.

A case in point was "The Glenwood Madam," Shirley Simnick, who authorities said ran a lucrative prostitution ring from her south suburban home.

Shirley claimed her escorts modeled lingerie and stripped for bachelor parties but did not engage in prostitution. Simnick apparently ran a tight ship and employees who failed to toe the line would face Shirley's wrath. During her 1991 trial prosecutors told the court that Simnick exercised complete control over her girls even to the extent of fining escorts fifty dollars for having chipped nail polish.

Testimony at the trial was spicy and the courtroom of U.S. District Judge Harry Leinenweber was filled most every day with spectators. What made the trial a cut above most prostitution cases were the undercover audio and video tapes that were played in court by the government.

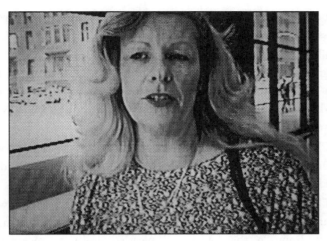

Shirley Simnick, "The Glenwood Madam," ran lucrative prostitution ring from her south suburban home.

On one occasion Shirley had called all her girls to attend a "council of war" at a south suburban motel. Simnick decided to have the summit meeting after learning she was under investigation by the FBI.

Unknown to Shirley one of her employees, was cooperating with the government, and wore a concealed tape recorder. After calling the meeting to order Shirley announced she was being investigated by the Feds. Then Shirley, sounding like a head football coach, gave her girls a pep talk:

"We are at war, we can lose it or we can win it."

"How can we win it, Shirley?" one of her employees asks.

Shirley snapped back, "by everybody sticking together."

Later on the tape Shirley counsels an escort who was afraid that her mother might find out what she was doing. This was Shirley's advice:

"You're going to have to deny it, you're gonna have to lie, girl, 'till the day you die."

Court buffs were treated to videotapes of undercover FBI agents meeting escorts in suburban motel rooms. The tapes were secretly recorded by other agents who were stationed in an adjoining room. The hidden camera had been placed in the room where the assignation was taking place.

The scenario usually went like this. After engaging in small talk and after the agent paid a sum of money. The escort would then begin to disrobe. But, before the tape could get X-rated police would come crashing through the motel door and the escort would be arrested.

The court buffs may have eaten it up but it didn't turn on all the jurors. After five days of deliberations the jury remained deadlocked and the Judge declared a mistrial.

The Justice Department planned to try the "Glenwood Madam" again. But before the second trial could get into high gear Shirley threw in the towel and pleaded guilty to racketeering charges. Her guilty plea came about after her attorneys and the Justice Department worked out a deal.

Shirley never went to jail. She was sentenced to one year of house detention. She had to forfeit her Florida home and also forfeit one hundred and three thousand dollars that prosecutors said she had obtained illegally.

Although prosecutors had wanted Shirley to do time, the Judge took notice of Simnick's deteriorating physical condition. Shirley Simnick was a sick woman. She had cancer and it was terminal.

Two years after her 1992 sentencing hearing Shirley Simnick succumbed to cancer. She was forty-eight years old.

JIMMY NICHOLAS, SAY HELLO TO ROSIE

James "Jimmy" Nicholas was a member of the Rocky Infelise street crew which was indicted by the Federal Government in 1990. Nicholas, a forty-seven-year-old soldier with the crew, was never charged with any "hard stuff" such as murder, conspiracy, and extortion.

Nicholas was a gambler by profession. He liked the horses, cards, and just about any kind of action that came down the pike. He was no palooka when it came to gambling. Nicholas was reputed to be the gambling boss of Greektown.

The Mob liked "Jimmy" because it considered him a "stand up guy." That assessment stemmed from the time Nicholas refused to testify before a Federal grand jury that was investigating the activities of Infelise and some of his cohorts. Nicholas reportedly was rewarded, allegedly receiving one thousand dollars a month from Infelise, for keeping his mouth shut.

But Nicholas wasn't a candidate for canonization either. According to prosecutors, Nicholas would lure gamblers to card games by offering them the availability of prostitutes. Federal agents said Nicholas wasn't providing female companionship, just to be a "Good Time Charlie." The Feds said those card games, that "Jimmy" was running were rigged.

One thing to be said for Nicholas, the girls he supplied to his card playing clientele were strictly high class. No street walkers for "Jimmy." In fact, government undercover tapes revealed that Nicholas dealt with the "Gold Coast Madam," Rose Laws, who operated one of the premier call girl rings in Chicago.

*Rose Laws, the "Gold Coast Madam" leaves the Criminal Courts Building.
Rose was in good spirits when this tape was shot.*

Fortunately for posterity's sake, the first meeting between
Jimmy and Rose was recorded. It came about at the Lake Shore
Drive apartment of William "B.J." Jahoda, an associate of Infelise,
who had become a government informant. Jahoda's apartment was
wired for sound on that Saturday morning in September of 1989
when Rose came calling.

Nicholas was trying to line up some companionship for his
clients and he found out that Rose would be willing to supply a
number of winsome lassies, if the price was right. We begin our scenario as Jahoda lets Rose into his forty first floor apartment:

Jahoda: "Jimmy Nicholas, say hello to Rosie."

Nicholas: "Rosie, the famous Rosie. How are you Rosie?"

Laws: "I don't want to be famous. Some people do."

Jahoda: "Here, sit over here."

Laws: "We have some gorgeous girls. We have models. We have ah,
Penthouse, Playboy girls."

Laws: "...but now, the way we operate, just so we understand. What
keeps me in business is, I can't guarantee a particular girl at any time
ever. The way I operate, if this girl breaks her leg and your second
choice has got her period, and your third choice's grandmother died,

I still have your fourth choice. In other words, I guarantee you a beautiful girl, but I don't guarantee you a certain girl."

Jahoda: "Well, Beauty is the in the eyes of the beholder."

Nicholas: (inaudible) "Within reason on the prices, Rosie."

Laws: We're two hundred and fifty the first hour for one girl. And one hundred and fifty the second hour, and it's not negotiable. It's the rate."

Nicholas after assuring Rose that his clientele is not riff-raff tells Laws he doesn't want any surprises when her girls come calling. Nicholas indicates that price is not a factor. He says that each girl will get a "nickel" apiece, that's five hundred dollars in layman's terms. But Nicholas stands by his guns, he wants to inspect the merchandise before forking over any money.

Nicholas: "…Bring me three girls. I want to see, I don't want no surprises. I'm going to look someplace else, too. And I'm gonna hand pick. Whoever gets, whoever accommodates me, gets my business. You know, you know I want to be fair."

Laws: "It's fair."

Nicholas: "If you be fair with me, I'll be more than fair with you. I'm a nice friend to have. Let's put it this way. You can take that to the bank."

It appeared that everything was coming up roses for Laws. However, we don't know for sure if Nicholas and Rose completed their business transaction.

As for "Jimmy." He soon had other business on his mind. Less than five months after his conversation with Laws, Nicholas was indicted. In 1991 Nicholas pleaded guilty to gambling and criminal contempt charges. Two years later, Nicholas was sentenced to serve four and half years in a Federal prison.

Laws also ended up in a courtroom. But Rose, a matronly appearing woman of sixty, never went to jail. In October of 1993, Laws pleaded guilty to charges of conspiracy to pimp and conspiracy to keep a house of prostitution. She was sentenced to eighteen months of conditional discharge. That's a fancy name for a form of probation.

When Laws' case was finally disposed of, there were many sighs of relief. Rose's clients reportedly included judges, a prosecutor, politicians, and a number of entertainment and sports figures. The Cook County States Attorney's Office went to great lengths to make sure Rose's customers were never publicly identified.

Rose, an excellent saleswoman, swore off the escort racket. She turned her attention to running her Loop flower shop on a full time basis. In her last court appearance, Rose was admonished by her sentencing judge, Thomas Durkin, who told Laws:

"I hope the only romance you will be involved in, will have to do with selling flowers."

THE COLONEL'S WIDOW

Often a simple phone call is all that is needed to set up a story. But that's not always the case. Sometimes lengthy negotiations are necessary before the subject or subjects involved in the piece give their consent to be interviewed.

That's what happened when we did a story for our "Chicago Chronicles" series on Maryland McCormick, the widow of one of the most powerful publishing figures in U.S. History. Her second husband was Colonel Robert McCormick, the legendary and controversial publisher of the *Chicago Tribune.*

When we approached Mrs. McCormick about doing a story, the Colonel had been dead for twenty four years. Although Mrs. McCormick was at first reluctant to go on camera and talk about her ex-husband, she later changed her mind. You see, it sometimes pays to be persistent.

I had grown up a *Tribune* reader and had heard all sorts of stories about the Colonel, a colorful character, if there ever was one. I was eagerly looking forward to our session with his widow. And I wasn't to be disappointed as Maryland Mathison McCormick, a former society belle from Baltimore Maryland was as outspoken as her late husband.

We interviewed Mrs. McCormick in her luxurious East Lake Shore Drive apartment that was filled with impressionist paintings. She gave me and a Channel Two news crew a tour of her lovely residence. Then we sat down and had a long chat.

The Colonel and Maryland were married during World War II when he was sixty four and she was forty seven. It was the second marriage for both. He was a widower and she was divorced.

Maryland and her first husband, Henry Hooper had separated in May of 1944 and were divorced later that year. In asking for a Mexican divorce, Maryland had charged her husband with drunkenness.

In December of 1944, four days before Christmas, Maryland married the Colonel, a man admired and respected by some but hated and feared by others. But Mrs. McCormick told us that stories about her husband being some kind of ogre weren't true. She claimed the Colonel had more bark than bite: "They were frightened of him. No reason to be. He had a lot of compassion. He had a rather austere way with him which I think may have been on account of his height, which frightened them."

The McCormicks were married for only eleven years. But they weren't an ordinary couple. There were the fox hunts at Cantigny, the McCormick estate near suburban Wheaton. There were the endless parties, with the McCormicks playing host to VIP's from various walks of life. And then there were the many trips overseas the couple made in a converted bomber.

After the war McCormick bought a surplus B-17 flying fortress bomber for the bargain basement price of just fifteen thousand dollars. The plane was completely renovated. The gun turrets and the bomb bays were removed and beds and chairs were installed.

The plane was re-named the "Chicago Tribune" and was used by the Colonel to barnstorm around the world. McCormick and his spouse would visit world leaders and check out the overseas Bureaus run by *Tribune* correspondents. Maryland McCormick fondly remembered the days when she and "Bert," as she called the Colonel, were world travelers:

"They were wonderful, they really were. We traveled all over. We carried a crew of five. We met Juan Peron and Evita, the King and Queen of England. We were treated like royalty. We knew all of the lords of the Press. We knew Beaverbrook (Press Baron Lord Beaverbrook), we knew them all."

Colonel McCormick was a lifelong Republican but he had nothing but contempt for what he called the "internationalist, me-too wing" of the party. That faction of the GOP Was led by former New York Governor Thomas E. Dewey and a number of other prominent eastern republicans.

In 1952, McCormick was a strong backer of Senator Robert Taft of Ohio, while the Dewey faction of the party supported General Dwight Eisenhower, the eventual nominee.

Mrs. McCormick told us that when she and her husband visited Ike's NATO headquarters outside of Paris in early 1952, the Colonel pledged his support to the General if Taft did not get the nomination.

Mrs. McCormick said Ike was in top form and flattered the Colonel when the couple came calling. Maryland said the meeting between her husband and the general remained etched in her mind:

"Eisenhower turned on all his charm which is considerable. Ike recalled that at one time we had the same maid. 'Bertie" told Ike, 'I'm committed to Taft but if you get the nomination I will support you.'"

That tidbit from Mrs. McCormick was a news story. The Colonel reportedly had told his inner circle, before the convention, that he had not made up his mind on whether to back Ike if he got the GOP nod. Yet, Mrs. McCormick told us that "Bertie" was willing to accommodate Eisenhower, the champion of the eastern wing of the party, a good six months before the convention.

Eisenhower not only got the nomination but won in a landslide over Illinois Governor Adlai Stevenson in the November election. We never did find out McCormick's assessment of the Eisenhower era. The Colonel died in 1955 and Ike had only been in office a little over two years.

When we interviewed Mrs. McCormick in 1979 she was eighty two years old. She was vivacious, as sharp as a tack, and had a great sense of humor. The Colonel, legend had it, was an austere, autocratic man without much of a sense of humor. He needed someone like Maryland Mathison to keep him in tow and bring him down to earth once in a while. I think she was the perfect match for her husband.

THE MUSKIE LADY

It's the biggest, the meanest, and the most elusive fresh water game fish, the mighty muskellunge, officially known as Esox Masquinongy, commonly known as the muskie. The muskie has a torpedo shape with a sloping snout filled with razor sharp teeth. No wonder the muskie is nicknamed "the tiger of the lakes."

Many anglers will spend a lifetime without ever boating one of those lunkers. Yet, in downstate Mattoon, Illinois, there is a middle aged woman who has not only caught legal sized muskies but bagged a muskellunge the first time she ever went muskie fishing. Her name is Sylvia James and by profession she's an educational consultant who works with handicapped children. In the Northwoods though, fishermen know her as the "Muskie Lady."

After reading about Sylvia in a Chicago publication, "The Outdoor Notebook," we got hooked on the story and headed down to Mattoon to interview Sylvia. You see, female muskie anglers with a few exceptions, have been until very recently about as rare as hen's teeth.

Sylvia told us from the den of her Mattoon home that she was christened the "Muskie Lady" by an envious fellow angler at the Lake of the Woods in Canada.

"He just kind of pointed in my direction and said 'you know that's the lady you need to watch, that's the Muskie Lady. She really catches them. They like her.'"

Not only did Sylvia catch a muskie her first time out but for three years in a row she hauled in a muskie on her birthday. These were legal size muskies Sylvia was catching. The minimum for a legal size muskie, depending on the state or lake you're fishing, can run anywhere from 32 to 40 inches or more. That's a real big fish.

Sylvia James — "The Muskie Lady" — caught a legal size muskie her first time out.

Sylvia's husband Bob, a veteran fisherman, takes a lot of kidding from his buddies. They tease him about his wife's prowess with as rod and reel. Bob James though says the joshing doesn't bother him:

"I love it, I love it. She's a pretty grand lady." And Bob James gets off the hook by claiming he's responsible for part of his better half's success. Bob says he guides his wife to where the fish are.

Legend has it that it takes ten thousand casts to catch a legal size muskie. That may not be gospel but for a muskie novice like Sylvia to hit pay dirt right away. But it was quite an accomplishment. Granted there is some luck involved. However, if the reader feels that boating a muskie the first time out is no big deal go out and try it. The odds are the only thing you'll have to show from your baptism under fire is a sore back.

The reader may wonder why people like Sylvia spend long hours in a boat casting heavy lures all day for a fish that is very difficult to catch. Sylvia admits she's puzzled about it herself:

"The challenge is just incredible. I enjoy doing it. But I don't always understand why I stay out there for twelve hours and just cast and retrieve."

Muskie fishermen can be a strange breed always hoping, sometimes praying, that the next cast will produce a world's record. A 69 pound 15 ounce muskie caught in the St. Lawrence river back in 1957 is accepted in most circles as the current world's mark. Sylvia and hubby Bob say that on two occasions, a huge muskie played cat and mouse with their lures while the pair were trolling on a favorite Canadian lake. Like a true muskie angler Sylvia will never forget the moment when the big fish almost took her bait:

"I saw her twice, she followed a black bucktail. I don't think we could have ever boated her. I think we would have had to beach it. She was sixty to eighty pounds, at least. She was half the length of a seventeen foot boat...

If Sylvia ever lands that monster muskie she probably will have a world's record on her hands. Fame and fortune await her. But the odds of catching a muskie that large are very, very, slim. However, when you've been infected with "muskie fever" to the degree that Sylvia has, you'll never quit tossing those big lures. You always hope that on the next cast a huge lunker is going to grab that bait. Then it's hold on and "Katie bar the door."

CHAPTER SEVEN

Tough Guys

THE LAST MOMENTS OF BILLY DAUBER

When we videotaped William "Billy" Dauber leaving the Will County courthouse in Joliet, on a hot July afternoon in 1980, the husky hit man had less than an hour to live.

The forty-five-year-old Dauber, sources said, had been living in constant fear that he had been targeted by Mob assassins. He usually drove a van that was armored plated on one side. And according to several investigators, he often started his car by remote control.

Dauber was no shrinking violet himself. He allegedly told one underworld associate that he had killed thirty one people. That may have been a bit of exaggeration on Dauber's part. But there was no question that Dauber was a feared Mob enforcer responsible for keeping south suburban chop shops in line.

How many people Dauber murdered is open to speculation. His name surfaced in a number of slayings and he was even a suspect in the murder of his former boss "Jimmy the Bomber" Catuara. Dauber was a triggerman "par excellance, "one of the most vicious hoodlums in the crime syndicate's arsenal.

But the Dauber we encountered at the courthouse seemed subdued, almost resigned to whatever fate had in store for him. He didn't object when our camera zoomed in on him. He responded with polite no comments to my questions. The only thing Dauber said was "It's a nice day." This was in stark contrast to the Dauber we photographed approximately a year before in the same courthouse. Then Dauber got hot when he saw a crowd of reporters and cameramen waiting for him to exit the building. He gave a cameraman from Channel Five in Chicago a beautiful stiff arm, almost sending the photog sprawling to the pavement. The burly Dauber was so furious and frustrated by the media wolfpack that he flooded his car when he tried to start his late model Lincoln Continental that was parked by the courthouse.

We couldn't pass up using the shot of Dauber giving the straight arm to the photog. We teased the story on our six o'clock news. As the shot of Dauber lashing out at the cameraman appeared on the screen, our caption read "Billy Dauber meets the press."

Doomed hit man Billy Dauber leaves Will County Courthouse July, 1980 — flanked by attorney Ed Genson and author.

But there were no laughs for the feared Mob hitman in Joliet on July 2, 1980. Dauber was in court that day in connection with a drug charge. Nothing of substance happened in the courtroom and the case was continued.

But what was significant was that Dauber had become an informant and was cooperating with Federal law enforcement agencies.

His testimony could take a lot of people down. Authorities theorize that Dauber's Mob bosses got wind that Bill was talking to the Feds and ordered him killed.

"Whacking" Dauber, however, would be no easy matter. As we noted earlier Dauber drove a van that was partially armor plated. He was often accompanied by a gun toting bodyguard. And Dauber who was almost paranoid about a possible attempt on his life usually carried a weapon himself.

Investigators have told me that the killers were parked near the courthouse when Dauber and attorney Ed Genson, followed by a Channel Two news crew, left the building. Dauber and Genson went to a nearby doughnut shop where they were joined by "Billy's" wife Charlotte.

The Feds have told me that the killers were prepared to gun down Dauber on the street but opted instead to follow Dauber's car as he and Charlotte drove toward the couple's home near Crete. Apparently the hit squad felt it would be foolish to take Dauber out by the courthouse with so many potential witnesses around.

Ironically on the day of the murder the usually cautious Dauber was driving his new Oldsmobile and not the armor plated van that was his normal mode of transportation. Why Dauber opted to take the Olds and not the van has never been fully explained. Thus, Dauber and his wife were sitting ducks as they drove along a rural Will County road heading for Crete.

Police say the hit went down with military precision. One of the killer's work cars swerved in front of Dauber's Olds. While Dauber was frantically trying to avoid being forced off the road, another vehicle pulled along side firing a volley of shots at Dauber's Olds. Dauber lost control. The car went off the road and struck a tree.

Details about the murders of Dauber and his wife came to light nine years after their deaths. Mob hit man Gerald Scarpelli confessed to the FBI that he was a member of the crew that killed the Daubers. Scarpelli told agents Jack O'Rourke and Tom Noble that he leaped out of his van and supplied the coup de grace. According to Scarpelli's statement he fired two or three shotgun blasts into

Dauber at point blank range. Charlotte who was in the wrong place at the wrong time was already dead, Scarpelli said.

Scarpelli told the FBI he was in the crew that killed Dauber and his wife.

Scarpelli implicated veteran enforcer William "Butch" Petrocelli and several other men in the murders. But nobody has ever been charged with the slayings. Petrocelli, himself was hit less than a year after the Daubers were murdered.

Shortly after his confession became public knowledge Scarpelli was found dead in a locked shower stall at the Metropolitan Correctional Center in downtown Chicago where Scarpelli was awaiting trial on interstate robbery charges. Jail officials said Scarpelli had committed suicide.

On the day of the Dauber murders we didn't realize that we had a major story on our hands until we got back to the station. The show producers said they had no interest in a routine court appearance by Dauber. But before I could get settled in my office the phone rang. The caller informed me "your friend got it today." About five minutes later an investigator from the Will County

Sheriff's department phoned me, saying that Dauber and his wife had been killed.

Who made that first call? I never found out. Perhaps it was another Sheriff's Policeman from Will County or perhaps it was one of Petrocelll's crew who saw me at the courthouse and wanted to crow about taking out the vaunted Dauber. We'll never know.

I couldn't resist pulling the legs of our show producers who didn't want to have anything to do with a Dauber story that day. I went into the newsroom to inform our people about Dauber's demise. The scenario went something like this:

Drummond: "What do you want to do about the Dauber story?"

Producer: "We told you before, nothing"

I replied that I thought the station should at least mention that Dauber and his wife had been murdered. The place went up for grabs. It was the biggest Mob slaying since Sam Giancana was liquidated in 1975. It wasn't just a TV story. The deaths of Billy and Charlotte Dauber rated headlines in both of Chicago's major newspapers the next day.

I often wondered what would have happened if our Channel Two news crew had followed Dauber on that fateful day. A courier had been dispatched to take me back to Channel Two where another assignment was in the works. Before leaving I radioed the assignment desk asking that our crew follow the Daubers to Crete. I had heard that Dauber had taken a lot of security precautions at home and I wanted to get videotape of the house. But the assignment desk said they had more important things for the crew to do. They were sent elsewhere.

So we'll never know what might have happened if a Channel Two minicam crew had appeared on the scene when Mobsters were getting ready to put the finishing touches on Dauber and his wife. Would the cameraman have gotten some exclusive footage of a Mob hit? Or would the crew be the first newsmen to have been slain, gangland style, in the Chicago area since Jake Lingle was murdered in the early 30s?

I told crew members "Skip" Brand and Greg Jackson that it would have been a no lose situation for them. They either would have come away with some award winning footage or their loved ones would be able to collect on the double indemnity clause in their company's life insurance policies. Besides I said, "we're all expendable." I'm afraid the crew didn't find my comments very amusing.

THE COLLECTOR

John Cannatello was in the juice loan business, a collector for a Chicago street crew headed by "Jimmy the Bomber" Catuara. His clientele included gamblers, drug addicts, fences, and small businessmen who couldn't get loans through normal channels.

Cannatello claimed business was so good in the early 1970s that he had eight men working for him. His team made loans of three to five thousand dollars at anywhere from ten to twenty percent interest a week. In some parts of the country such a practice would be called loan sharking or shylocking. But in Chicago loans with exorbitant rates of interest are known as juice loans. The interest on the loan being the juice payment. The Mob doesn't worry when the principle will be paid off as long as it get it's weekly juice.

When we interviewed Cannatello, a burly two hundred and fifty pounder, John told us he usually had little trouble getting juice payments from recalcitrant debtors.

"We would just politely ask him if he was gonna pay. As long as he paid the interest, nothing to do with the principle, as long as he paid the juice every week, that's all that mattered."

Cannatello said that when interest on the loan wasn't paid on time, other steps were taken:

"You'd just have to put a little pressure on him. Maybe you'd flatten his tires and if he didn't get the hint from that, slap him around a little bit, and if he really welshed and didn't get the hint, then you'd do a real number on his knees or his elbow or whatever. Then he knows pretty much what he has got to do. He's got to come up with the money.'

*Mob juice loan collecor John Cannatello, interviewed by the author.
A Louisville Slugger made debtors "see the light."*

We then asked Cannatello to elaborate on what he meant by a real good number: "…using a Louisville slugger and give him a whack on the knees and everytime he sits down, he knows that he didn't pay and he's got to pay."

Cannatello rationalized that his customers knew what they were getting into when they went to him for a loan. He argued that his clients were aware of the facts of life:

"They wanted the money bad enough. They knew the terms of the deal."

We met Cannatello in 1978 and by that time he had little to show for his halcyon days. He claimed he blew his nestegg by cabareting and drinking. He was no longer living high off the hog. Cannatello said he had no problem being a juice loan collector. But he said when word filtered down from his bosses that he should branch out into drug trafficking, that was another story.

John says he got into hot water with his Mob superiors when he skipped to Arizona without their okay. For a time things worked out for Cannatello in the Sun Belt. He claimed he scored with a scam or two. But it wasn't long before he got a message from his former underworld colleagues in Chicago indicating that they were real upset by his Arizona move. That pushed Cannatello over the brink. He went over to the other side and became a government informant, a rat in the eyes of his onetime associates.

But his honeymoon with the Feds didn't last too long. The FBI dropped Cannatello like a hot potato when he tried to shake down a Tuscon union official that he had been assigned to inform on. That meant Cannatello was up a creek without a paddle.

Things got worse. A dead pigeon with two pennies in it's beak was found at the home of his mother. Cannatello began running scared, constantly looking over his shoulder. He began talking like he was doomed:

"They buy their own time and their own thing. It can be seven years, it can be two years, it can be whenever. But if they want you, they got you. I can't blame them, I just hope they don't do a number on me, that's all."

Asked to elaborate, Cannatello replied that he preferred what he thought was the lesser of two evils: "I don't think I'd mind getting shot."

The onetime juice loan collector expressed fear that Mob muscle men might pour gasoline on him and burn him bit by bit. That Cannatello defined as a "real number."

Our 1978 interview with Cannatello was the result of lengthy negotiations. Cannatello was willing to do a television interview if certain provisions were met. We were not to show his face on the screen and we were not to reveal his real name. We called him "John Conti" when we aired the story. Another provision, Cannatello insisted upon, was that I would talk to the head of the FBI's organized crime squad in Chicago to see if a repentant Cannatello could get back into the witness protection program. We tried but the Bureau wasn't interested. The FBI felt that Cannatello had let them down real hard when he blew his cover in Arizona by attempting to muscle the union official. The Feds wanted nothing to do with the guy.

Cannatello had another reason for making a quick trip back to his old home turf in Chicago. He had a close relative living in the

Chicago area that he hadn't seen for some time. So it finally worked out for both parties. We agreed to pay his air fare to Chicago and back, two night's lodging in a hotel, and moderately priced meals during that thirty six hour time frame. He received no cash or gratuities for the interview, just expenses.

On the morning of the scheduled interview I received a frantic call at home from our overnight assignment editor, Gera-Lind Kolarik. Cannatello was upset and threatening to pull out, Kolarik said. He had checked into a Lake Shore Drive hotel where Channel Two had reserved a room for him. But Cannatello didn't like the room or the hotel. He wanted to be upgraded to a hotel on Michigan Avenue, the Westin. If he didn't get his way, Cannatello warned, he was heading for the airport where he would take a plane back to the west coast.

We gave in. Cannatello checked out of his hotel and taxied over to the Westin where he said he got a "nice room." We didn't know it then but we had a real tiger by the tail. Cannatello started spending money like it went out of style. The best scotch, steaks, you name it. The bellhops got a real workout making a number of runs to Cannatello's room. You name the culinary delight or the best in booze, they brought it to John. Cannatello obviously liked the good life and since he was spending CBS's money why wouldn't he.

When the hotel called the station to tell the news department about the bill Cannatello was running up, we put the kibosh on any more room service. I had a hunch that since Cannatello would be picking up his own tab, from then on, his tastes would be more frugal.

It was hard though not to like Cannatello. He was an engaging guy who made an excellent interview. The audience liked it, perhaps because he looked and sounded like he was the real McCoy. Although we didn't show John's face we made shots from the back as he walked down the street.

Cannatello had gone a little bit to paunch but he was still a husky guy. No wonder he had little trouble collecting on his juice loans.

We didn't run the interview until Cannatello had left Chicago for parts unknown. But as soon as the two part series had aired, we got a couple of phone calls. The callers knew who our mystery guest was. The phone calls went like this "who are you trying to fool, Drummond? That guy you call John Conti, used to hang out around 29th and Wallace. We know all about that guy. His name isn't Conti, it's John Cannatello."

I don't know what happened to John Cannatello. A few years ago I got a call from a man who said that Cannatello had gotten into a jam in the Bay Area of California. According to the caller, Cannatello was involved in some kind of scam. But he didn't want to go into detail.

I wish John well and hope he stays out of trouble. It's possible he made amends with his former pals. But I doubt that. As one investigator put it, several years after we did the Cannatello profile, "John is between a rock and a hard place, he's got nowhere to go."

THE NEW ALCATRAZ

It doesn't fit the image of the big house that Hollywood depicted in the 1930s and 40s. There are no high walls surrounding the U.S. Federal penitentiary at Marion. In fact, the prison has a very scenic setting, since it is located on the edge of a lush national wildlife refuge in southern Illinois.

Yet, the penitentiary at Marion was known for years as the toughest prison in America. Some called it the "New Alcatraz," others referred to it as the "New Rock." But many of it's inmates called Marion the "House of Hate" or the "House of Pain."

Marion became operational in 1963, the same year that Alcatraz, a bleak island fortress in San Francisco Bay was closed. Alcatraz, the subject of numerous books and movies, housed the nation's most hardened criminals.

Marion was not originally designed to be the "New Alcatraz." That came about after the Bureau of Prisons set up a new security classification system. All Federal prisons were rated from one to six, with the higher numbers denoting the most secure. Marion was the only prison to be designated a number six.

By the mid 1970s the makeup of the Marion population began to change. As one prison official put it, "They started putting all the rotten apples into one barrel." That barrel turned out to be Marion.

In prison parlance, Marion was a place where hard men did hard time. In most cases prisoners sent to Marion were considered incorrigible, troublemakers, security risks, and the most escape prone. Others ended up at the Southern Illinois Prison because they were too hot to handle anywhere else. Very few inmates were sent to Marion directly. They came from other institutions where prison officials were eager to get rid of them.

There were exceptions. Mafia boss John Gotti, some drug kingpins, spies, and a few others were assigned to Marion right after sentencing. But, by and large, most inmates don't end up at Marion unless they screwed up somewhere else.

It was only natural that penologists and others would try to compare Marion and Alcatraz. Gary Henman, a veteran with the Federal prison system, was the warden at Marion when we interviewed him in 1987. Henman felt Marion housed more dangerous inmates:

"If you take a look at a cross section of the typical inmate that was housed in Alcatraz compared to ours, there's just no comparison. Our inmates by far have much more assaults in their background. They have a higher level of murders and longer sentences. There are just more aggressive types of individuals than you would have normally found in Alcatraz."

When a visitor arrives at Marion, a cursory look can be deceiving. As we pointed out earlier, the prison is not surrounded by huge walls of the Atlanta or Stateville mold. The facility can almost pass for a college complex. I say almost, because a closer look brings the visitor back to reality.

You won't forget the rows of razor sharp concertina wire on top of two twelve foot high chain link fences that surround the prison. That razor wire can lacerate the flesh even at the slightest touch. And you don't forget the eight guard towers where sharpshooters are armed with a variety of weapons.

By penitentiary standards it is not a large prison. The inmate population, at the time we did several stories there, was around three hundred and fifty. Marion, with it's tight security, guard to prisoner ratio, and remote setting would appear, on the surface at least, to be escape proof.

But, in October of 1975, five prisoners did the impossible. They broke out of Marion. The five escapees literally walked out the front door of the prison, after one of the ringleaders circumvented a security panel that opened three electronically locked doors.

The elaborate escape had been planned for a year. One of the desperadoes, Edward Roche, worked in the prison's electrical shop. He put together an ingenious device similar to a TV remote control box. The device jammed the guards' closed circuit TV camera while opening the electronic doors at the same time. The prisoners walked out casually, while a member of the Williamson County Historical Society was giving a lecture in the lobby of the administration building.

In 1975 there was no guard tower by the main entrance to the prison. The escapees ran up a hill and disappeared into a mist that had enveloped the area that night. When the guards realized that an escape was in progress they hit the floodlights. But the mist made it difficult to pinpoint the fleeing convicts. They had dashed into the dense woods of the Crabtree Wildlife Refuge.

The escape by the five inmates triggered one of the biggest manhunts in Illinois history. At WBBM-TV, management galvanized it's troops quickly. I, along with a film crew, was dispatched to the small downstate community of Salem, where a police command post had been set up.

An armada of law enforcement types was all over the place. FBI agents, Sheriff's deputies, state police, U.S. Marshals, auxiliary cops, you name it, even tracking dogs got into the act. It seemed anybody who wore a badge was on the scene. Roadblocks were set up on the interstate, as well as on secondary roads, and even dirt roads. The authorities ordered all freight trains that passed through the area to maintain a speed of at least fifty miles an hour. That way the escapees would not be able to hop a moving freight car.

Some farm families moved into town to stay with friends or relatives rather than risk an encounter with the desperadoes. Other farmers sat up all night with shotguns at the ready in the event the convicts might come calling.

And the escapees, described by the FBI, as extremely dangerous, did come calling. Two of them made their way to a farmhouse about twenty miles from Marion. There, they tied up an elderly couple and fled taking a car and some guns.

But police soon spotted the stolen car and a high speed chase ensued. But the chase ended five miles east of Salem when the two convicts lost control of their vehicle and it crashed. One of those apprehended was Arthur Mankins who was doing time for the murder of an FBI agent in North Carolina.

A total of five men had broken out of Marion on that Friday night in October. By early Tuesday three were back in custody, including Edward Roche, the electronics wizard.

That left two men still at large. One of them was Henry Gargano of Chicago who was serving a one hundred and ninety nine year sentence for killing two suburban Northlake policemen during a bank robbery in 1967. At the time of the escape, authorities considered Gargano one of the most dangerous convicts in the Federal prison system. He was thought to have been the ringleader of the escape.

The forty-five-year-old Gargano was something of an escape artist. In 1964 he fled from a prison camp at Lewisburg, Pennsylvania where he was doing time for an earlier bank robbery. Then after the Northlake bank job, he tried to escape from the Metropolitan Correctional Center in downtown Chicago. But that was foiled.

Gargano, in a published interview, described the Northlake bank shootout as a fire fight "like in Vietnam." He told the reporter he didn't feel any remorse for the two dead cops. Gargano, himself, was shot in the Northlake score. When apprehended at a cabin in Indiana several days later he reportedly told lawmen that if he had not been wounded and weak, the cops would not have been able to take him alive.

There was no question that the large contingent of police officers were concerned about Gargano. That was obvious after a farmer said he spotted one of the fugitives in his cornfield. The lawmen, wearing flak jackets with shotguns at the ready, surrounded the section of the cornfield where the convict, presumably Gargano, supposedly was hiding.

A helicopter was brought to the scene, and while the 'chopper hovered very low Over the field, a cop on board shouted through a bullhorn for the escapee to surrender. Despite all the heavy artillery, nobody seemed eager to march into the cornfield and shoot it out with the man believed to be Gargano. The long standoff ended when it was obvious that Gargano or the other missing "con," Dennis Hunter had slipped away.

A day after the cornfield incident Gargano was seen walking along some railroad tracks in southern Indiana. He had somehow slipped through the police perimeter and had hopped a freight train.

But, Gargano who lawmen thought would shoot it out, if cornered, surrendered meekly.

"I'm the guy you're looking for," Gargano told the police. The fugitive later explained why he threw in the towel so quickly. He contended that he was exhausted and weak after going several days without food or water.

Gargano paid for his few days of freedom. He spent a year and a half in the "hole" and had five years added to his sentence.

The fifth and last of the fugitives, Dennis Dale Hunter, a convicted kidnaper, was apprehended in Winnipeg, Canada twenty days after the escape. Hunter had made his way to Chicago where he commandeered a taxicab and went on a wild ride through the city. The cabbie said Hunter kept a knife at his throat before jumping out of his taxi. That was the last reported sighting of Hunter in Chicago.

The twenty-six-year-old Hunter next turned up north of the border where he was picked up and returned to Marion to face the music.

We never had an opportunity to talk to any of the fugitives immediately following their capture. They were strictly off limits at the time. But twelve years later we did a lengthy interview with one of them, Arthur Mankins. Mankins, a lifer, was no virgin when it came to busting out of jail. Mankins ended up at Marion after fatally shooting an FBI agent who was trying to apprehend him because he had escaped from a North Carolina prison.

It didn't take much to persuade Mankins to discuss the 1975 Marion breakout. He grinned and spoke with obvious relish as he described the escape.

Mankins, a "lifer," broke out of Marion in 1975. He is shown here recounting the daring escape to the author.

"That was good. I think it's the best escape I've ever had any part of. I think it's the best escape I ever heard of, because it went off so smooth. There wasn't even a shot fired. The people here didn't even know, we was gone. I didn't believe myself that the door was open. It surprised me, it really surprised me that the door was open."

But Mankins who was forty nine years old when we talked to him in 1987 seemed resigned to spending the rest of his life in prison:

"I don't think the Feds are ever going to turn me loose. Like my lawyer told me when the thing happened in '73. He said 'the only thing you could have done worse would be to kill the President' you know that's how bad it really is."

Mankins never left Marion. I was told recently by prison authorities that Mankins had died. But officials would not reveal any details about Mankins' death.

The Gargano crew was the last to break out of Marion. There

were other attempts including a bizarre incident in 1978 where a woman hi-jacked a helicopter and landed on the grounds just outside the prison. The woman was shot by the pilot and the plot failed.

Escape attempts were not the only problem facing Marion officials. Following a series of killings at the prison, authorities implemented a number of strict security measures. In effect, the prison was placed under a virtual lockdown with most of the prisoners confined to their cells for twenty three hours a day.

Officials at Marion have noted that the number of homicide and assault cases have been reduced significantly since the lockdown went into effect in 1983.

From February of 1980 to October of 1983, nine convicts and two guards were killed. In that same time frame there were also a number of mini-riots, fifty seven assaults, and thirty three assaults on prison employees. Since the lockdown went into effect in 1983, no staff members have been killed.

Although Marion officials called the lockdown necessary for the safety of inmates and staff, prison reform groups were sharply critical. A Quaker organization, the American Friends Service Committee, called conditions at Marion, brutal repression.

One inmate, John Greschner, a convicted murderer from Minnesota described conditions at Marion as "explosive."

Greschner made the comment when we interviewed him at the prison in the late 1980s.

"The people, here at Marion are creating animals. They're creating a very, very, bad situation."

Despite predictions by inmates such as Greschner and others that Marion would explode. There have been no major disturbances of the kind that rocked Attica and several other penitentiaries.

Marion can no longer boast that it's the toughest prison in America. That dubious distinction now belongs to a Federal penitentiary in Florence, Colorado. Marion, though, is still a tough "pen." It has it's share of hardened criminals. It has not, as one official put it, been turned into a "country club."

PUBLIC ENEMY NUMBER ONE

To his friends and co-workers at a Deerfield Beach, Florida warehouse he was known as Robert J. Niewiadomski. But the husky thirty-five-year-old who loaded trucks for a Florida supermarket chain was in reality a Federal fugitive, Jack Farmer. Authorities had called Farmer one of the most vicious criminals in Chicago annals.

Farmer's sojourn in the Southland ended in the late spring of 1988, shortly after he became Public Enemy Number One on the FBI's Ten Most Wanted List.

Farmer had been profiled on the television show, "America's Most Wanted." Police, acting on a tip from a viewer who recognized Farmer as Niewiadomski, arrested Farmer and his wife Pamela outside of the couple's rented home in Lantana, Florida. Farmer and his thirty-seven-year-old wife had been fugitives for more than a year. The twosome had left Chicago in spectacular fashion. Farmer's 1987 escape from custody was one of the most bizarre cases of a guy going on the lam.

Farmer, described in newspaper headlines, as a "cocaine czar" or "drug lord" was being held at the Metropolitan Correctional Center in downtown Chicago on charges of racketeering, violation of drug laws, and income tax violations. Farmer, a suspect in two murders, was accused of being the head of a gang known as the "Little Mafia" which terrorized residents in a West Side neighborhood of Chicago, called the Ukrainian Village.

While awaiting trial, Farmer was given permission by the Court to confer, with his attorney at the lawyer's loop office. The meeting took place without any guards or U.S. Marshals present. Farmer couldn't resist such a golden opportunity to escape. Lawyer Alan

Blumenthal told police that the two hundred and twenty pound Farmer tied him up with his own necktie and gagged him with his trenchcoat belt. Then Farmer did the quick change act, switching from jail garb to street clothes, apparently supplied by his wife. Farmer then sped away in a car driven by the faithful Pamela. Investigators believed the escape had been planned well in advance.

Jack Farmer made FBI's Ten Most Wanted list.
He committed suicide in prison.

Street talk had it, that not only were lawmen looking for Farmer and his spouse during their thirteen months of freedom, but that the Chicago Mob had also placed Jack on it's "most wanted list." Reportedly the Outfit was sore because Farmer had been posing as a crime syndicate figure in his drug and juice loan deals. The story went that Farmer wasn't paying any street taxes and that his activities were putting heat on the real Mob.

The tale that Mobsters had a contract out on Jack was never confirmed. It became a mute point after Farmer was apprehended in Florida.

In the fall of 1988 Farmer, his wife, his brother, and six alleged members of his gang, went on trial. I don't recall any other case at the Dirksen Federal Building where there were so many U.S. Marshals or court security personnel on hand because of one single defendant. That defendant, escape artist and self proclaimed tough guy, Jack Farmer. There have been other cases, such as the FALN and El Rukn trials, where heavy security, including metal detectors was evident. But that was because of a multitude of defendants and possible trouble from associates of the defendants. In the Farmer trial, it was Jack that authorities were concerned about.

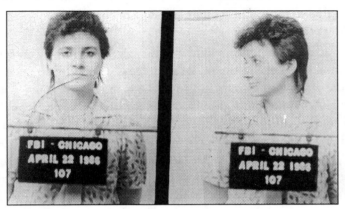

Pamela Farmer helped her drug czar husband Jack escape from a lawyers office.

When prosecutor James Schweitzer outlined the government's case against Farmer and his confederates, the veteran assistant U.S. Attorney, was playing to a full house. Word had spread that the Farmer trial would have what one court buff described as "drama at it's best."

Schweitzer was in private practice in Milwaukee at the time of the trial. But he went "TDY," that is temporary duty, with the Justice Department to try the case. Schweitzer had strong feelings about the defendants calling them, "one of the most vicious groups of people I have ever seen in my years with the U.S. Attorney's Office."

Spectators in the courtroom of Judge James Holderman heard a sordid story of murder, home invasion, drug dealing, and terrorism. Although authorities said Farmer had brutally killed one man and had a role in the death of another, he was not charged with murder. That's because such a crime was not covered by Federal statutes. Farmer had been tried earlier in a state court on a murder charge but was acquitted. During his Federal trial prosecutors said Farmer had bragged that he had fixed a 1982 murder case by paying his lawyer forty five thousand dollars to bribe the judge.

Prosecutors introduced secretly recorded audiotapes where Farmer was heard talking about "blowing up the house" of a rival drug dealer. He was also caught on tape talking about robbing and killing others in the drug business.

Although the audio tapes were very damaging to Farmer's defense, it was the testimony of a homeless man that turned out to be the government's smoking gun. The man told the court that he saw Jack Farmer put a pistol to the head of a suspected would be informant while two of Farmer's henchmen held the hapless victim. Witness Kent Fisher's straight forward testimony captivated both the jury and spectators. Fisher said the 1982 incident occurred outside of an abandoned warehouse near skid row. Fisher testified that the victim, identified as Al "Maniac" Norris begged for his life. But according to Fisher, the man's cries for mercy went unheeded.

Fisher said he heard Norris say to Farmer, "No, Jack no, I've got your money." But Fisher said that Farmer shot Norris anyway. Although Farmer wasn't being tried for murder, Fisher's testimony gave the jury an insight into Jack's character.

If Fisher's testimony wasn't enough, Farmer helped dig his own grave by talking about the Norris murder to a former member of his gang, Taras Jaworskyj. Jaworskyj had gone into the witness protection program and was singing for his supper. In May of 1983 Jaworskyj was wearing a concealed tape recorder as he and Jack Farmer drove around the Northwest Side. That's when Farmer began boasting and laughing about the demise of Norris. Norris, behind on his drug payments, had threatened to inform on Farmer's narcotics activities. Norris' threats to blow the whistle sealed his doom. Farmer began describing Norris' death throes as Jaworskyj's tape recorder took it all in:

Farmer: "...He was like a jelly bowl. Boom, boom, boom, boom (laughs) that's how his body was going, like a jelly bowl."

Jaworskyj: "Always got room for Jell-O."

Farmer: (laughs) "I think I hit a fuckin' artery or something, making fuckin' all kinds of blood come out and shit."

Jaworskyj: "All things, yeah, so it starts squirting."

Farmer: "That would have been nasty if fuckin' the shit would have squirted all over me.

(Both laugh)

In December of 1988, two days before Christmas, Farmer got bad news from the jury. He, along with his wife Pamela, his brother, and four other defendants were convicted on a variety of charges. Two suspected members of Farmer's cocaine ring, including a former Chicago Police officer were acquitted.

Farmer got hot when the jury verdicts were read. Judge Holderman ordered Farmer removed from the courtroom after Jack began talking loudly to his lawyer or to anybody who would listen. It was the first time at the Federal Building that I could remember when a defendant had gotten the heave ho when he was found guilty of a criminal charge. But you could see that Farmer was doing a slow burn and was about to go off the deep end if he hadn't been surrounded by U.S. Marshals.

Three months later, under very heavy security, Farmer was sentenced by Holderman. But before sentence was pronounced, Farmer addressed the court telling the packed courtroom that prosecutors and the press had made him out to be something that he wasn't. Said Farmer: "Schweitzer and his bag of thugs, and TV and the press, convicted me. I didn't get a fair trial."

Judge Holderman disagreed, sentencing the one time drug baron to forty years in prison. Farmer could have gotten as much as ninety two years or as little as twenty three years.

Prosecutor Schweitzer, who wanted the maximum, appeared upset and quickly left the courtroom as soon as sentencing was pronounced. Schweitzer told me and other reporters that day, that he feared for his life. Said Schweitzer about Farmer: "he will be a model prisoner and get out and come after me and Kent Fisher." Fisher you may remember was one of the key government witnesses at the trial.

Schweitzer's concerns proved academic. Farmer never got out of jail to get anybody. In June of 1993, four years after he was sentenced, Jack Farmer was found hanged in his cell. Farmer had been doing time at the Leavenworth Federal penitentiary in Kansas, which is no country club. Prior to his death, Farmer reportedly had been having some problems with other inmates. He had been placed in isolation for his "own protection" after some fellow convicts had beefed that he was stealing drugs.

Authorities said Farmer's death was a suicide. He was forty one years old when he died. His wife, Pamela, was doing a twenty year stretch, at another Federal prison when Jack did the "Dutch Act."

Jack Farmer was a big story at one point. But by 1993, he apparently had become passe as far as the news media was concerned. His demise attracted little attention other than a short obit in the newspapers.

MOB MUSCLEMAN

When James LaValley became one of the "good guys," prosecutors netted one of the more articulate witnesses to ever take the stand at a Chicago Mob trial. LaValley, a burly six foot, two hundred and twenty pounder, wasn't the kind of guy who frequented ice cream socials. LaValley, authorities said had a mean streak in him that made him a natural when it came to terrorizing individuals who had aroused the ire of the crime syndicate's honchos.

Like a baseball player who learns his trade in the minors, LaValley earned his stripes, first as a burglar, then as a street hoodlum, and finally as an enforcer for the Chicago Outfit. By the time LaValley was in his early 40s, he was a Mob muscleman and a good one. He had all the ingredients for the job. He was big, had a swagger, and not only looked menacing, but actually was. He worked for upper echelon Mobsters such as Gus Alex and Lenny Patrick. LaValley's job was to persuade recalcitrant debtors that it was in their best interests to see the "light."

Unfortunately for LaValley, his escapades did not go unnoticed. His notoriety piqued the interest of the FBI and Chicago Police. It didn't take investigators long to come up with the names of some of LaValley's clients. And one of them, a fifty-five-year-old gambler was, very eager to get LaValley off his back. He agreed to wear a wire when he met his brawny antagonist.

It seemed that the gambler had a little larceny in his heart. The gambler had been placing bets with an operation headed by one of LaValley's buddies, a minor player with a bookmaking ring. The man, a clerk in the ring, had been inflating the aforementioned gambler's winnings in exchange for a piece of the profits. When

Mob higher ups found out that they were being cheated, they sent LaValley out to rectify the situation. LaValley, in no uncertain terms told the hapless gambler that he had to pay back all the money that he had won. That amounted to over a hundred grand, no small piece of change.

James LaValley changed his black hat for a white one.

The gambler who we will call debtor number three, his FBI code name, was wearing a concealed tape recorder when he met LaValley at a suburban River Forest gas station on July 23, 1988. That conversation was recorded for posterity. The tape of that discussion was played in open court and got heavy play from the media. And with good reason. The tape was very dramatic.

The gambler was heard begging for mercy as he was being worked over by LaValley. It was a David and Goliath confrontation. But debtor number three, was only five foot four inches tall and had no slingshot.

LaValley began the conversation by trying to intimidate his victim. He demanded to see debtor number three's drivers license. A veiled threat that LaValley and his associates needed his home address in case the victim needed more coaxing. What follows here is a transcript of a portion of the conversation that was played in the courtroom:

LaValley: "Give me your license, your drivers license."

Debtor # 3: "Why?"

LaValley: "Give me your drivers license. What do you have to know for?"

Debtor # 3: "No I don't want to. (starts screaming) oh, oh please, please. Please."

LaValley: "Get back over by the car. I'll just fuckin' stab you right here."

Debtor # 3: "I know, I believe you."

LaValley: "Give me your fuckin' license you cock sucker. If you ever talk to me like that again."

Debtor # 3: "Please."

LaValley: "Who do you think you're talking to, a fucking asshole?"

Debtor # 3: "No. Please"

LaValley: "You scream like a fuckin' cunt."

Eventually debtor number three takes his drivers license out of his wallet and hands it over to LaValley. But his tormentor continues to threaten his diminutive victim. The victim promises to pay back all the money. But that didn't appease LaValley. Then debtor number three brings up his mother in the conversation, telling LaValley that his mother is seriously ill. However, that didn't dissuade the crime syndicate enforcer:

Debtor # 3 : "You don't believe that my mom has got cancer. I got problems."

LaValley: "Listen you cock sucker. You got problems the day you cheated us."

Debtor # 3: "I didn't cheat you. Oh. Oh God."

LaValley: "The next time you. Move over here."

Debtor # 3: (crying)

LaValley: "Come over here. What did I tell you about telling me you didn't cheat on us."

Debtor # 3: "I'm sorry."

LaValley: "You (inaudible) cheatin' on us didn't you?"

Debtor # 3; "I'm sorry, you broke my nose."

LaValley: "That's good."

The gambler was given a codeword to use if he thought he was in danger of death or serious injury. He never used it, according to Federal agents and cops who were parked near the gas station, monitoring the conversation:

The incident with debtor number three was not the only time that enforcer LaValley was unleashed by his masters. According to court testimony LaValley burned one victim with a lighted cigarette and on another occasion had slashed the hand of a suburban bartender who owed the boys four thousand dollars.

But it was the dramatic audio tape that probably convinced LaValley that he should be wearing a white hat and not a black one. He pleaded guilty to extortion charges and began cooperating with authorities. LaValley's decision to start "singing" stunned his underworld compatriots who thought the onetime enforcer was a standup guy.

By the time LaValley appeared before Federal Judge Brian Duff at a sentencing hearing he had already testified for the government at several Mob trials. Duff said that LaValley may have given himself a death sentence by informing and testifying against some of the Chicago Outfit's top leaders. Said Judge Duff at the July, 1992 hearing: "I think you've given yourself a death sentence, if anyone finds you. And that will be true even behind prison bars."

Although Duff described LaValley's crimes as calculated and brutal, the Judge, a Korean War veteran, gave the former Mob muscleman a back handed compliment: "In a certain way you are an impressive man...If you'd been next to somebody on a battlefield, they'd been awfully glad you were there."

Prosecutors Chris Gair and Mark Vogel also praised the defendant. Gair described LaValley as a "powerful witness for the government." But Gair warned that LaValley would be a walking target in public. "When he hits the street and he will someday, he is a dead man. His life is changed and it will never be the same."

LaValley was sentenced to a term of seven years and seven months in prison. Obviously LaValley never spent that hitch as an inmate in the general prison population. Informants who are key witnesses or potential witnesses in forthcoming trials don't mingle with other cons. That would be too dangerous. In fact they don't do time in the strictest sense at all. They are usually stashed away at some location where they are interrogated by investigators looking for fresh information. In other instances they are periodically briefed by prosecutors about an upcoming trial in which they (the informants) will be called upon to testify.

LaValley took the stand in cases involving Mob bigwigs, Gus Alex and Rocky Infelise. His testimony also helped convict a bookmaker crony, James Ballman, even though LaValley appeared in that trial as a defense witness.

There are those in the legal community who believe that the Federal Government has gone overboard in allowing thugs and other criminals to "skate" because they are willing to testify against their former bosses. The argument goes that the witness is more dangerous or has committed more serious crimes than the man the Justice Department is trying to put behind bars. Prosecutors don't buy that. They argue they would be hard pressed to gain convictions against bad guys without the cooperation of former "rotten apples" who have seen the errors of their past ways.

Be that at it may, LaValley was an excellent witness for Uncle Sam. He had an excellent memory, could recite detailed accounts of incidents involving his former Mob confederates, and stood up well under cross examination. He also looked the part. No Casper Milquetoast type, LaValley obviously impressed jurors that he knew what he is talking about. Although well dressed, LaValley projected an image of a Mob insider. In fact he looked like he came out of central casting.

The Justice Department won't say what happened to LaValley. We assume he is in the witness protection program. But I think it's safe to say that he no longer hangs his hat at his old Chicago haunts where the welcome mat is no longer out.

CHAPTER EIGHT

For Armchair Sleuths

Everybody loves a good mystery and most everybody is an armchair sleuth. People are not only fascinated by unsolved homicides, heists, and missing person cases but usually have strong opinions as to who the culprit was. Often in covering a murder case someone would come up to me, on the street, and say "The husband did it or the boyfriend did it." You get the idea, people love to play detective.

That's why there will always be a market for mystery novels, who dunnit TV shows and movies. Murders that haven't been solved, big scores, where the loot hasn't been recovered, and missing persons cases have been a fertile field for the media. Long before the TV show "Unsolved Mysteries" became a nationwide staple, local television stations parlayed unsolved police cases that had occurred in their communities into a marketable item.

In the early 1970s, Channel Two news took a number of high profile Chicago murder mysteries and made a five part series about them. Although you don't want to go to the well to often, we would periodically resurrect other unsolved murders and package them. In just about every instance, viewer feedback was favorable.

Sometimes police departments are not always eager to cooperate on such episodes. That's because some cops feel they look bad since they have been unable to solve the case. But usually, with a little arm twisting, the police will go along and open their files for you.

On a lean newsday editors can always fall back on their files for murders and missing person cases that had occurred on the same date. The first, fifth, or tenth anniversaries of such cases give you some kind of newspeg. For example, how many times have Chicagoans read about the disappearance of State Representative Clem Graver, Graver vanished and was presumably kidnapped on June 11, 1953. No trace has ever been found of the lawmaker and it's believed he was murdered although his body was never recovered. If there is not much happening around the tenth of June and editors are looking to fill space, you can be sure that a reporter will get out the dusty Graver file and rehash the story once again.

Television does the same thing. For a time, you could always be sure that at least one local Chicago station would do a story on the anniversary of candy heiress Helen Vorhees Brach's disappearance.

Producers are on firm ground with this kind of story. There may not be any new angles but the public never seems to get tired of hearing or reading about them. By the same token, the piece can be productive from an investigative point of view. A witness or a friend of a suspect might decide to "drop a dime" and provide police with new information about the case. That has happened when someone, his or her conscience bothering them, decides to own up. If nothing else, an anniversary piece sometimes provides new leads, although it must be conceded that those leads usually don't pan out.

Speaking of mysteries, I've always been intrigued as to what happened to Ruth Steinhagen. The reader will probably mutter, "Who the blazes is Ruth Steinhagen?" You ask former major leaguers or scribes who covered the diamond sport right after the war, and they'll tell you. Ruth Steinhagen would be called by today's jargon, a baseball groupie.

Ruth had her fifteen minutes of fame in the late 1940s when she shot Philadelphia Phillies first baseman "Cowboy" Eddie Waitkus. In happened in May of 1949 when the Phillies, in Chicago to play the Cubs, were staying at the Edgewater Beach Hotel. Steinhagen apparently had a crush on Waitkus who had formerly played with the Cubs. Waitkus though, told police he had never seen Steinhagen before that fateful night. The "Cowboy" said he was lured to the woman's room where the shooting took place.

Detectives said Steinhagen's bedroom, in her Chicago home, was something of a Waitkus shrine. There were pictures of Waitkus plastered all over the walls. After finding out that the Phils would be staying at the Edgewater, Steinhagen checked into the hotel.

Waitkus told police that when he returned to his room after eating dinner with another former Cub, Bill Nicholson, he found a note from Steinhagen telling him she had something important to tell him. When Waitkus came to Steinhagen's room, the young woman took a rifle out of a closet and shot the baseball player through the lung. Steinhagen then calmly picked up the phone and told the operator that she had shot a man. The Steinhagen-Waitkus scenario was dramatized in the movie "The Natural." Robert Redford took the part of the diamond star in the fictionalized version of the shooting.

Although Waitkus was seriously wounded he recovered and played Major League Baseball again. Steinhagen never elaborated as to why she wounded the first baseman. She just told police that she "had to shoot Waitkus." Ruth Steinhagen was judged insane and was committed to a mental institution. She was later released, I was told, but nobody knows what happened to Steinhagen after that. Finding Steinhagen would be a great "Where are they now story." Unfortunately we could never deliver on that one.

A writer could do a whole book on unsolved mysteries in the Chicago area. In fact it's been done. Such a tome was compiled by a couple of veteran police reporters. We are making no attempt to duplicate those efforts here.

Instead we've selected a cross section of cases that are becoming to accumulate some dust but are not yet ancient history. They are solvable though and in some instances may be cleared in the near future. The cases we selected haven't been getting a lot of ink recently and in some ways are as fresh as new mown hay. One is a missing persons case, another was a big heist and there are a couple of murders. So Sherlockians put on your Deerstalking cap, light your pipe and lean back in your armchair. Maybe you can come up with a clue that will help the police clear the case.

THE BLIZZARD MURDERS

Sometimes a major news story doesn't get a lot of play because something more significant occurred that same day. That's what happened on the cold winter night of January 11, 1979 when the bodies of three northwest suburban residents were found slain in a farmhouse in northwest Cook County.

Normally a triple murder in the suburbs is a headline story. But that wasn't the case in the deaths of Earl and Elizabeth Teets and their son Gary. All three had been shot to death. Earl Teets who was sixty years old had been shot in the chest. His wife Elizabeth who was also sixty had been fatally wounded in the neck. Their thirty-five-year-old son Gary had been shot in the heart.

Channel Two News broke the story of the murders on it's ten o'clock newscast with what is called in the trade, a reader. A reader contains no video or sound bites. The anchorman, reported from the set that Sheriff's Police were on the scene at a farm near Hoffman Estates where three people had been found shot to death.

That was all the information that was available at the time. But we had a camera crew on the site. The crew had video taped the bodies being carried to an ambulance. They also had shots of the back of the farmhouse where the trio had been killed, video of the general area, and an interview with Lt. Frank Braun of the Cook County Sheriff's Police who was in charge of the homicide investigation.

In other words we had geared up for a follow up on the story for the next day. We assumed that the murders would get heavy coverage in the late editions of the *Tribune, Sun-Times,* and *Daily Herald.* We also assumed that the three murders would be the lead story on the morning drive time radio newscasts.

But it didn't turn out that way. A blizzard slammed into the Chicago area that night and by the time it stopped more than twenty inches of the white stuff had fallen. That snowstorm triggered a siege of savagely cold weather. The winter of 78-79, as Chicagoans well remember, was brutal. From the standpoint of cold and snow it was the worst winter that the city had seen since the Weather Bureau started keeping records.

The bottom line was that the Teets murder, not only got knocked off the front page. It got very little coverage at all. The story was not only forgotten by the media but the weather hampered the work of investigators by making it very difficult, if not impossible, to search the property for clues and evidence.

Detective Tom Smith of the Cook County Sheriffs police said the weather put the brakes on an intensive investigation: "It seemed like bad luck was against us from the beginning of the case. The snow was definitely a problem...It blanketed the area for a period of about two months and we weren't able to actively find any physical evidence in the area at that time."

With more snow storms, a perpetual cold wave, and a heated mayoral campaign, the Chicago media paid little attention to the Teets investigation. There were few, if any, follow up stories. Although some law enforcement people don't like the spotlight of publicity on their investigative efforts, most lawmen concede that newspaper stories and radio and TV reports about a crime often result in citizens coming forward with information about the case.

But with a dearth of news about the triple slaying, those kind of sources dried up. The weather and the news blackout didn't deter detectives from proceeding with their investigation. But it was rough going. Even after interviewing family friends, business associates, and neighbors the police had little to go on. Some people were given lie detector tests. But nothing conclusive came out of those polygraph examinations.

There was no sign of forced entry to the farmhouse and police worked on the premise that the killers were known to the Teets family. Investigator Smith said there was no indication of a struggle: "It appears as though there was a discussion that turned into an argument. The argument became heated and the perpetrators pulled weapons and shot the family."

Slain farmhouse family. Son Gary at left with parents Elizabeth and Earl Teets.

Ballistics showed a 38 caliber revolver and a 9 millimeter automatic pistol were the murder weapons. One of those guns was also responsible for the death of one of the family's four guard dogs. A German Shepherd was found shot to death in the living room. A second guard dog had been locked in a bed room while two others were found in a shed behind the farmhouse.

To this day the motive for the triple slaying remains unclear. Authorities don't believe the killers went to the farmhouse to rob the family. Investigators recovered six thousand dollars in cash that had been rolled up in a sock and left in a dresser drawer. Other money was also found in the house by lawmen. In addition, police say, a number of expensive figurines were not taken by the killers when they left the scene.

One theory advanced by sleuths, shortly after the murders, was that the triple slaying was a case of mistaken identity. Police said a large amount of marijuana was found at another farm in the area.

Could the killers have stopped at the wrong farm house to consummate a drug deal? Police say there is no evidence to link the Teets family to any kind of involvement in narcotics.

The Teets property was used by a private towing company for a temporary storage site for vehicles that had been abandoned or damaged. Could the killer have come to the Teets farm to reclaim his car only to be rebuffed? Could a heated argument over a car on the property have escalated into a shooting? Investigators don't think so. The Teets farmhouse had been ransacked. But police don't know what the killers were looking for.

A fifteen thousand dollar reward was offered for information about the murders. However, the reward failed to develop any solid leads. A psychic was even brought in. But that proved fruitless.

Eight months after the triple slaying, an arsonist torched two barns on the property and the ramshackle farmhouse. Investigators, though, don't believe the fires were connected to the murders. The Teets farm is no more. The land is now part of a forest preserve.

The murders of Earl, Elizabeth, and Gary Teets remain unsolved. Periodically new investigators are assigned to review the case. But police apparently are no closer to clearing the three murders than they were that cold January night when a blizzard hit the Chicago area with it's full wintry force.

THE MURDERED EXECUTIVE

Unlike the murders of the Teets family, the slaying of oil company executive Charles Merriam got plenty of coverage. The Teets case went on the media back burner when a blizzard slammed into the Chicago area, literally burying the Teets story.

But there were no snow storms or severe weather in Chicago when the fifty-two-year-old Merriam was gunned down in the doorway of his northwest suburban Prospect Heights townhouse. Merriam was shot to death on November 4, 1987 and his murder made headlines and was a lead story on local TV newscasts. The Merriam murder was a high profile case. It was what they call a "heater."

Charles "Chuck" Merriam came from a very prominent Chicago family. His uncle, Robert Merriam, a one time Chicago Alderman, ran against Richard Daley in the 1955 mayoral race. His father moved in the best social circles and was a successful patent attorney. And his grandfather was a famous political science professor at the University of Chicago. With that kind of pedigree, and the circumstances surrounding his death, it was no wonder that the Merriam murder was a big story in Chicago.

Charles Merriam didn't opt for the legal, academic, or political arenas when he graduated from DePaw University in 1956. Instead he went to work for what was then called Standard Oil of Indiana. At the time of his death he had spent thirty one years with the oil giant, that is now known as Amoco. He rose through the ranks of Amoco, from an entry level position to District Marketing Manager. In that post he was in charge of some one thousand Amoco stations in Illinois, southern Wisconsin, and northwest Indiana.

Murdered oil company executive interviewed by Channel Two News.
His slaying was a hit, investigators said.

His job put Charles Merriam in the hot seat. His responsibilities included informing full service station owners that their facilities would have to be converted to self serve mini-marts. This did not sit well with some station owners who had no desire to go the mini mart route.

Another of Merriam's assignments was to discipline station operators for violating Amoco policies. He also had a role in determining what stations should be closed. It's logical to assume that Merriam made some enemies in his job but basically, he was only carrying out the directives of the company. Friends and associates told investigators that Merriam had received threats that were connected to his job.

In reconstructing the crime scene, detectives said that Merriam, who was separated from his wife, was preparing for bed when someone rang the door bell. Merriam's town house was located just off the grounds of the Rob Roy Golf Club. When Merriam opened the door, police believe words were exchanged before the victim was shot in the chest. Merriam was shot two more times before the killers fled. Investigators feel that there were two assailants, since two guns were used in the murder, a 380 caliber pistol and a 25 caliber automatic.

A witness told the Sheriff's department of seeing two men exit a car that was parked in Merriam's driveway. The witness said that the men left the engine running as they approached the townhouse. According to the witness, apparently a neighbor, an argument ensued and shots were fired.

Why did Merriam open the door? One theory was that Merriam knew at least one of the men. But some investigators have dismissed that scenario. Instead sources have told me that they believe the killers wore either police uniforms or were garbed in the uniform of a private security service.

The two guns used in the slaying were never recovered. Divers probed a pond on the Rob Roy golf course but only found some golf balls that had ended up in a watery grave. The Cook County Sheriff's Police went over the crime scene and immediate area with the proverbial fine tooth comb. They even looked at a number of sewer openings but came up empty handed.

Police have long ruled out robbery as a motive. There was no indication that anything of value was ever taken. The killers never entered the house and fled immediately after the shooting.

Sources believe the killers were paid to "hit" Merriam and did not have a personal beef with him. Investigators feel that the murder had something to do with the victim's business dealings and not his personal life. A one hundred thousand dollar cash reward was offered by crime stoppers and Amoco for information leading to the arrest and conviction of Merriam's killers. But the reward apparently failed to provide any significant leads.

The Cook County Sheriff's Police filled a filing cabinet with information about the case and more than twelve hundred people have been interviewed. Although the lengthy investigation has not resulted in any arrests or indictments, detectives remain confident that the murder eventually will be solved.

Lieutenant Len Marak who was the detective first assigned to the Merriam slaying said police have no intention of throwing in the towel: "time is on our side now because murders don't go away. Somebody did it and as long as these people are still out there, there's a good chance we'll find out who they are. It might not be today, it might not be tomorrow, but it can happen."

Other investigators have told me they believe they know who killed Merriam, and why. But they can't prove it. Detectives say three men are ptime suspects in the case.

THE MARLBOROUGH DIAMOND

A story about the theft of an egg sized diamond from a ritzy London jewelry store may seem out of place in a chronicle involving Chicago characters, but a jewel mystery in "merry old England," had a Chicago angle.

The two robbers who pulled off the score turned out to be Chicagoans, Joseph "Jerry" Scalise and Arthur "The Brain" Rachel, a couple of underworld warhorses.

The September, 1980 robbery at Graff's jewelers, in the fashionable Knightsbridge section of London, was well executed. The pair had apparently cased the exclusive jewelry store before the heist went down. Scotland Yard inspectors said that the daring daylight robbery, which occurred on one of London's busiest shopping streets, took less than a minute. Lawrence Graff, the owner of the jewelry store said: "They (the robbers) knew exactly what they were looking for."

The loot valued in 1980 dollars at three point six million included the 45 carat Marlborough diamond. According to store owner Graff, the Marlborough diamond had a retail value of nine hundred and sixty thousand in American dollars. In addition to the Marlborough diamond, two pendants and twelve other jewels were taken in the heist. The Marlborough diamond, which was once owned by one of England's most distinguished families, was the showpiece of the stores' collection of fine jewelry.

Store employees described the robbers as two well dressed white males who were mustachioed. Fred Marsh, a uniformed guard, at the store told London police that he opened the door for what he thought were prospective customers. Then Marsh explained that one of the robbers took out a revolver and pushed it against him. "He (the robber) said 'this is a robbery' and that "he would shoot me if I didn't stop looking at him.""

This egg-sized diamond was the showpiece in Graff's collection of fine jewelry.

One inside the jewelry store, one of the men pulled out, what appeared to be, a hand grenade. Police said later the device might have been a smoke flair rather than a grenade. But whatever it was, it did the trick. Five store employees and two customers hit the deck in a hurry. The bandits scooped up the jewelry and walked out of the store with swag valued at more than three million dollars.

It looked like the perfect score but then things began to quickly unravel for the bandits. The thieves had made a couple of critical mistakes. Those miscues proved to be the undoing of the bandits.

An observant twenty-six-year-old London accountant provided Scotland Yard with some key information. The accountant, Colin Protheroe and his girlfriend were strolling down the street moments before the robbery. Protheroe felt that something was "rotten in

Denmark" when he noticed that a false beard, worn by a man later identified as Art Rachel, detached itself from Rachel's chin. Protheroe followed the two men and when he saw the pair put on white gloves as they entered the store, the accountant knew something was up. When the two bandits walked briskly out of the store Protheroe wasn't far behind. He followed the two suspects until they reached their rented car. The amateur detective wrote down the license number of the vehicle and called police.

Scotland Yard got into the act. They traced the rented Fiat to a Hertz agency in London. Surprisingly both men had used their own names in renting the car. And in another blunder, the two Yanks did not use aliases in registering at a hotel.

According to court documents, the employees at Hertz advised Scotland Yard that the car had been rented to an Arthur Rachel of 1020 Ardmore in Chicago and a J. J. Scalise. The rental agreement for the car indicated that both Rachel and Scalise were staying at the Mount Royal Hotel. When yard detectives checked out the hotel, lo and behold, both men had registered under their own names. The room clerk told investigators that both men had been guests at the Mount Royal since September 4th. The robbery went down on September 11th.

Next on the agenda was a check of the airline manifests at Heathrow airport. The police hit paydirt. Scalise and Rachel were on the manifest for British airways flight 298, departing London at 2:15 P.M., London time. The flight was due to arrive at O'Hare field at 4:45 P.M., Chicago time.

The yard contacted the FBI in Chicago and when the plane landed, the Feds were on hand to welcome Scalise and Rachel back home. The late afternoon arrival of the two suspects was convenient for CBS. We were able to provide the story and tape of the plane in time for the evening news.

Federal agents and Scotland yard were delighted that they had nabbed Scalise and Rachel at the airport. Agents and customs went over the men and their luggage with a fine tooth comb. But they found nothing to link the two Chicagoans to the heist. George

Mandich, then spokesperson for the Chicago office of the FBI put it bluntly: "there were no goodies on them, no weapons, no jewelry. A thorough check of the suspects, their luggage, and the plane turned up nothing."

Both Scalise and Rachel weren't out of the woods. Witnesses identified the pair as the robbers. So the sixty four thousand dollar question facing investigators was, what happened to the jewelry, particularly the Marlborough diamond?

The two suspects fought extradition back to the United Kingdom where they would face trial. But it was futile. At a magistrate's hearing in Chicago Assistant U.S. Attorney Gary Shapiro summed up the two defendants career's this way: "Their rap sheets read like a who's who in burglary and robbery in the U.S. ...There is considerable evidence linking them to the robbery (Graffs)."

Scalises' case wasn't helped by the testimony of FBI agent Joe Brennan who said Scalise was a suspect in five gangland murders and a string of armored car robberies dating back to 1966

Scalise and Rachel were represented at the Chicago extradition hearing by veteran defense attorneys, Ed Genson and Sam Adam. The colorful Adam, in an interview with this writer, theorized that the culprit was not either Scalise or Rachel but the notorious Professor Moriarity, the arch rival of Sherlock Holmes. Since both Moriarity and Holmes are fictional characters, Scotland yard didn't buy Adam's hypothesis.

The men were sent back to England where they were tried and convicted. In 1984 the defendants were sentenced to a fifteen year hitch in a British jail.

The trial did nothing to clear up the mystery of the stolen jewelry. But police have this explanation as to why the two men were "clean" when they were searched at O'Hare Field.

This much is known. Scalise and Rachel abandoned their rental car and took a taxi to the airport. Police say that on the way to Heathrow, the cab stopped at a post office where Scalise mailed a package. Scotland Yard believes that the package was mailed to a New York address. During the trial a British postal clerk, under hypnosis, recalled that the package given to him by Scalise to mail was destined for New York. Authorities are convinced that the package contained not only the Marlborough diamond but the rest of the swag as well. As of this writing none of the loot has ever been recovered. Police have theorized that the package was sent to a relative of the robbers or one of their underworld associates. Scalise and Rachel aren't talking about it, that's for sure. In fact, they've denied ever being involved in the robbery.

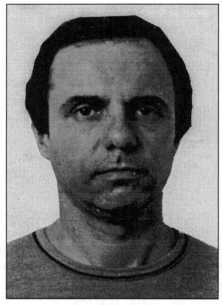

Joseph "Jerry" Scalise almost pulled-off "the perfect score" with Arthur Rachel. — a daring daylight robbery of a fashionable London jewelry store.

In 1988, while "Jerry" was in prison, we negotiated, with his attorney Anne Burke, to do an interview with her client. For a time it appeared that the interview was a go. According to Mrs. Burke, Scalise would consider talking about serving time in an English jail, his extradition to the United Kingdom, and his robbery conviction. Any discussion of the robbery itself, was off limits.

But the interview never materialized. "Jerry" apparently had a change of heart. Perhaps Scalise's reluctance to chat may have stemmed from the fact that he was getting a lot of play in the media at that time. In 1988 the FBI and state police had dug up two bodies a short distance away from a home in the southwest suburbs where Scalise once resided.

Arthur "The Brain" Rachel.

Scalise and Rachel did their time and came back to the states. Scalise was released in December of 1992 while Rachel was let out a month later.

But the mystery of what happened to the Marlborough diamond and the other gems taken from Graffs continues to baffle sleuths. A London insurance company offered a one hundred and twenty thousand five dollar reward for information leading to the return of the 45 carat Marlborough diamond. No one has collected on that reward.

Authorities can't rule out the possibility that the Marlborough diamond was fenced and sold intact to a private collector. Investigators though, don't believe that was the scenario. Police have opined that the diamond would be too "hot" and that even the most unscrupulous collector would be unwilling to pay a large sum for such a risky investment. The consensus among law enforcement now, is that the diamond was cut up and sold.

Investigators believe that the rest of the gems may have been sent to Las Vegas where the late Tony Spilotro was looking after the Chicago Mob's interests. At the time of the 1980 Graffs robbery Spilotro was running a fencing operation in Vegas. But the Spilotro angle is only speculation. There is no hard evidence to support it.

During a trip to London in 1996 I stopped at Graffs to see if someone at the store might shed some light on the Marlborough mystery. But a man who I assumed was the manager of the store was reluctant to discuss the robbery. He did, however, comment on the status of the Marlborough diamond. He believed, as do most lawmen, that the stone has been cut into several gems and disposed of.

The FBI and Scotland Yard haven't yet thrown in the towel on the Marlborough diamond. But time is running out. The mystery of the Marlborough diamond may never be solved.

WHERE'S WOODY?

I recall doing a story at the missing persons section in police headquarters. It seemed that the phone never stopped ringing. And no wonder! At that time, which was in the late 1970s, the department was investigating some twenty thousand cases of missing persons each year.

The vast bulk of those cases were cleared. The majority of those located were juveniles who had run away from home.

Most people who vanish do so of their own accord. There are a myriad of reasons why people decide to pull up stakes without telling a soul.

They can't take living with their spouse anymore. They're so heavily in debt that they can't see their way out. They're in hot water with the law and decide to go on the lam. In some instances they're just bored with life and want to make a fresh start somewhere else.

In most instances the disappearing act flops and the missing person turns up with egg on his or her face. But there are cases where foul play is involved and the missing person is believed to have been murdered, even though no corpse is ever found.

The 1977 disappearance of candy heiress Helen Vorhees Brach and the 1975 disappearance of former Teamsters boss Jimmy Hoffa would fall in that category. Much has been written and broadcast about the Brach and Hoffa cases. There is no need to go into them with any detail here. Certainly Brach and Hoffa did not fake their own disappearances. But when Woodruff Scoval Kelly Jr., AKA "Woody" Kelly vanished in June of 1985, that was a horse of a different color.

"Woody" Kelly was a forty-one-year-old investment counselor who on that fateful day had taken his forty two foot cabin cruiser "Piscator" out on Lake Michigan for a test run. Kelly had left Kenosha Harbor heading south to Waukegan, Illinois some twenty miles away. But he never made it to the Waukegan marina. The next day, June 9, 1985 the "Piscator" was spotted drifting aimlessly, close to shore, near Winthrop Harbor. When authorities beached the vessel they found no trace of "Woody."

Friends and associates of the missing man described Kelly as an experienced sailor. They said Kelly was no novice when it came to cruising around lake Michigan. There was speculation initially that Kelly who suffered from high blood pressure could have gotten dizzy or disoriented and had fallen overboard and drowned. But soon the thrust of the investigation went into a different direction. Authorities became convinced that Kelly had faked his own death.

Kelly's body never surfaced. No trace was ever found of the one time navy petty officer who had lived something of a Horatio Alger life. Kelly was a hail fellow well met type who would tell strangers and business clients alike to "call me Woody." Kelly's status as a fugitive, rather than a drowning victim, emerged after investigators began looking into his business dealings. Detectives theorized that Kelly had staged his own disappearance to avoid Federal prosecution and the wrath of clients he allegedly had defrauded.

At the time of his mysterious disappearance Kelly was feeling a legal noose tightening around his neck. Some three hundred investors, many of them senior citizens or working stiffs, had been smooth talked by Kelly into putting a good chunk of their hard earned money into his hands.

Three months after his June, 1985 disappearance Kelly was charged in absentia with mail fraud. An affidavit attached to the criminal complaint alleged that Kelly had failed to invest more than five million dollars that had been handed to him by his clients.

So the investigation switched gears. Lawmen all but ruled out that Kelly drowned. Instead they focused on Kelly as a fugitive from justice. "We are operating on the assumption that Kelly is still alive," said one FBI agent when asked about the Kelly case.

The charges against Kelly were little solace to the many small investors who had considered "Woody" a financial genius. They had bought Kelly's promises that he would win them handsome returns on their investments.

Mark Schoenfield, an attorney representing an insurance company involved in the case, said Kelly had good reason to disappear: "A lot of money. A lot of angry people. Law enforcement people have what is known in the trade as a slam dunk case for the prosecution."

There were several reported sightings of Kelly. Stanley Iwan, a deputy chief of the Lake County Illinois Sheriff's Department, signed an affidavit saying that he had seen Kelly at Busch Gardens, a Tampa Florida amusement park. Iwan, who said he had known Kelly, claimed he saw the missing man strolling about the amusement park. Iwan said the incident occurred in late 1990. The other "sighting" occurred in July of 1991. A Waukegan Fire Department captain told police that he spotted Kelly driving a Lincoln Town Car at a Waukegan intersection. Although both men seemed credible witnesses, Federal authorities took a dim view of the "sightings."

Seven years after his 1985 disappearance members of Kelly's family began efforts to have him declared legally dead. Kelly's former wife, Ann Proctor, who divorced "Woody" and remarried, filed a petition to have a judge rule on the missing investment counselor's status. If a judge declared "Woody" dead, it would mean that Proctor and the couple's three children could collect some four hundred and fifty thousand dollars in life insurance benefits.

But in February of 1994, Lake County associate Judge Emilio Santi refused the request of the family to declare Kelly dead. Judge Santi couldn't shed any light on what happened to Kelly but in making his ruling he told the family, "This leaves open the hope that maybe one day your dad and husband may finally reappear."

In the spring of 1994, the saga of Woody Kelly was featured on a national television show. More than one hundred viewers called with information about Kelly. But authorities said the tips turned out to be unproductive.

WOODRUFF SCOVEL KELLY, JR., aka
Woody Kelly, W/M,
DOB 10/4/43, 5'11", 200 lbs,
Brn/Blue; Occupation - Sales
Investment Advisor, Expert
Sport Fisherman & Boater,
Con Man;
Wanted by FBI, CG 196-2659,
Mail Fraud Warrant issued
9/20/85; Indicted 3/27/90
(NDI)

Kelly vanished in 1985, but investigators believe he's alive and well. Kelly is a Federal fugitive.

Kelly's family has said that "Woody" has never contacted them since that June day in 1985 when he vanished. Investigators though, remain convinced that the missing financier is still alive.

If Kelly is not deceased, where has he gone? Where is he living? What is he doing to make ends meet? Kelly never left any paper trail when it came to credit cards or cashed checks.

One investigator opined that Kelly was working as a charter boat captain in the Caribbean. Another thought "Woody" was living the life of an expatriate in Brazil. A more cynical detective had this assessment: "Wherever Kelly is, he's out there scamming, conning somebody out of some money."

THE CANON HEIST

It ranked right up there with the Purolater job and the Levinson jewelry store score, but the three million dollar theft at the Canon warehouse in west suburban Elmhurst never became a media darling. It got a little play in the papers and on the electronic media. However, the case never caught on and soon was placed on the back burner by editors.

Coverage of the 1979 murders of the Teets family was literally buried by a blizzard and a record cold wave. There was nothing of that consequence newswise that occurred in early August of 1978. Yet despite the usual summer doldrums the Canon theft never got much ink. That continues to puzzle me to this day. Veteran investigators say they could never figure out why the Canon heist remained, in effect, a nonentity in the world of journalism.

The burglary though, was big and very unwelcome news to the management at Canon, a Japanese company, which had it's midwestern headquarters and a warehouse in suburban Elmhurst. The warehouse contained expensive cameras, lenses, optical equipment and calculators.

The Canon heist occurred during an August weekend when there were no employees on duty in the warehouse. The burglary wasn't discovered until Monday morning when employees returned to work only to find that the facility had been looted. An inventory was taken and it revealed that some fourteen thousand calculators and more than five thousand cameras and lenses were missing. Elmhurst police Sergeant Pete Smith who headed the investigation and is currently the deputy police chief placed the retail value on the stolen loot at three million dollars. Those are 1978 dollars!

Elmhurst police, investigators from the Cook County Sheriff's department, and FBI agents swarmed over the Canon property grilling some one hundred employees. The lawmen then fanned out talking to people who worked in the neighborhood. They found out that a well known burglar, on the payroll of the crime syndicate, had stayed at a Holiday Inn adjacent to the warehouse. The man had spent several days at the motel in late July. Authorities came to the logical conclusion that the burglar had been in the area to case the warehouse.

Investigators believe the score went down after one of the thieves circumvented the building's alarm system that was wired to the Elmhurst police station. Then one member of the burglary team climbed to the roof of the warehouse and entered the building through a skylight, descending some seventy feet by rope to the warehouse floor. At that point he opened a door and let his confederates into the building.

From that point on it was a cakewalk for the thieves who had a field day inside the block long warehouse. Police said the burglars, probably numbering four or five, went through cartons of merchandise with a fine tooth comb. The intruders described by authorities as professionals, were selective in what they pilfered. They took merchandise that would be easy to unload on fences or underworld associates.

Conveniently for the bad guys an empty semi trailer had been left in the warehouse that weekend. The intruders placed their swag in the truck and drove away with no one the wiser. The burglars apparently took nothing from any of the offices in the building which also served as midwest headquarters for Canon.

Police examined many of the boxes containing merchandise that was not taken by the gang. Some of the boxes had been opened by the intruders but a check for fingerprints on the cartons was not productive.

An insurance company offered a fifty thousand dollar reward for information leading to the recovery of the stolen merchandise and the arrest and conviction of the thieves. If anybody ever collected the reward or a portion of it, the insurance company won't say.

A week after the burglary Chicago Police got a tip as to the whereabouts of the missing semi-trailer. Police recovered the forty foot trailer on the South Side. Although the stolen goods were long gone, invoices for some of the merchandise had been left behind by the thieves.

Investigators thought they had gotten a real break in the case when Sheriff's Police opened the trunk of a car they had stopped in suburban Maywood. The trunk contained three items that resembled some of the goods taken in the break in. Serial numbers on a camera and two calculators revealed that the items had indeed been stolen from the warehouse. The driver of the car and a passenger were charged with possession of stolen property. But the two men who were considered suspects, played it dumb when it came to the Canon heist. They were never charged with that crime.

Police armed with search warrants went to one of the suspects home in Chicago. But they found nothing there to connect him to the Canon score. The lawmen also visited another Chicago residence where they checked out a garage. They found no loot. Police had been told by an informant that some of the Canon swag had been stored in the garage. They found no Canon merchandise or for that matter any of the boxes that had contained cameras and calculators. However, investigators noticed impressions in the ground which they theorized had been made by boxes containing the stolen equipment. But nothing of evidentiary value was recovered at the garage site.

Later some of the stolen merchandise began turning up in the Chicago area. Police told me that a number of hot calculators were found on the desks of employees at automobile agencies and used car lots. But the recovery of the stolen calculators never led to any arrests.

An insurance company using undercover personnel did recover some of the Canon loot by buying it back from undisclosed sources. Those transactions, however, did not result in arrests or recovery of any significant portion of the stolen property.

The break in at the canon warehouse is still an open case. The Elmhurst Police Department has a thick file on the 1978 burglary. However, the odds of solving the theft grow slimmer with the passage of time. Authorities believe they know who was involved. But proving it is another matter. Still, investigators haven't conceded defeat, although the Canon affair is hardly a priority these days.

Cases with more cobwebs on them than Canon have been cleared. All it takes, as one police officer put it, is for somebody to "drop a dime." That could set the wheels in motion and the mystery surrounding the three million dollar whodunit might finally end up on the front page after all.

CHAPTER NINE

Attention Hollywood!

THE BALMORAL CAPER

Attention Hollywood script writers! Here's a story about a big score that didn't go down. But the aborted heist has the potential to make it on the silver screen. There was suspense, action, a touch of comedy, great dialogue, a bunch of characters right out of central casting, and a happy ending, because nobody got hurt.

Some called it the "Crime That Never Was," others described the scenario as another episode in the "The Adventures Of The Over The Hill Gang," while still others labeled the fiasco as the "Tardy Gang." That's because some of the crew showed up late for the job. Another label pinned on the would be desperadoes, was "The Super Cautious Gang." And last but not least, one wag called it the case of the "Reluctant Robber" because one member of the crew claimed he was forced at gun point to go along on the score.

Despite the blunders a gang of veteran burglars, some of them career criminals, almost pulled off a six hundred thousand dollar safe job at the Balmoral Race Track in south suburban Crete.

On the evening of November 28, 1983 a gang of burglars entered the racetrack grounds through an abandoned railroad tunnel. Once they were on racetrack property, they cut through a chain link fence to get to the grandstand area. There they circumvented the alarm system and at gunpoint overpowered two track security guards.

So far, so good. Everything to that point had been done with precision timing. The gang's target was a safe that they believed contained over a million dollars in cash.

In reality there was only six hundred grand in the safe. Not as much as the thieves thought but hardly chicken feed.

No doubt about it, it was going to be a big score.

Although the heist was botched, investigators said, the thieves had done their homework and came within minutes of pulling it off. Police said a lot of planning had gone into the Balmoral job. One of the gang members had worked at the track and was familiar with the whole operation.

Despite a game plan that on paper appeared perfect, the operation began to unravel. The snafu occurred when two of the robbers showed up at the scene late. That threw the all important timing of the job off. It forced the gang to flee before they were able to open the safe with a torch. One of the men who showed up late, was the gang's safecracker.

Although both track security guards had been bound and gagged, the thieves found out that more guards were about to come on duty. The bad guys knew of the shift change because one gang member had brought along a radio. That enabled them to monitor the frequency of the Balmoral security force.

When the would be safecrackers determined that additional guards would soon be arriving they decided that discretion would be the better part of valor. They hot footed out of Balmoral without even a penny of racetrack money.

Police said that if the two tardy gang members had been punctual the heist probably would have gone off without a hitch. Detectives also wondered why the robbers didn't wait for the two new guards to come on the scene and then ambush them and tie them up. That way, one investigator said, the gang could have gone ahead and completed the job. Well, it's easy to second guess. The bottom line, the gang opted to throw in the towel.

As it turned out, not getting any of the loot proved to be the least of the "super-cautious" gang's problems. It was all down hill after that. Things started to go awry in fleeing the scene. One of the getaway cars had a flat tire. Maybe there was a message in that.

Two of the thieves may have gotten bad vibes from the botched robbery before long they started "singing'" like the proverbial canary.

DiCaro was the mastermind of the Balmoral heist.

Five years after the aborted heist, seven of the eight suspected members of the Balmoral crew were indicted on conspiracy charges. One of them was Paul "Paulie" DiCaro, the alleged ring leader of the gang. He was very familiar with the track having worked there from 1981 to '83. Prosecutor John Scully said DiCaro, a south suburban resident, was the boss of the crew:

"This was his score, he was the mastermind."

Others charged with attempted robbery, conspiracy, and criminal use of firearms included Michael Gurgone, a city worker, who was identified as the gang's safecracker, Peter "Duke" Basile, a long-time underworld figure, Gerald "Bootsie" Ciancio, the gang's reputed electronics wizard, and Walter "Wally the Polack" Lesczynski. Lesczynski carried a rod and was supposed to do the heavy work. It was Lesczynski, authorities said, who pointed a gun at the two track security guards.

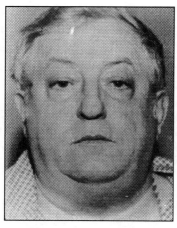

Thomas Harty, the wheelman, was the senior citizen of the Balmoral crew. Justice Department Photo.

Also indicted were Thomas Edward Harty, the wheelman, and a thirty-eight-year-old Chicago man who was found not guilty when the case went to trial.

Paul Panczko wore a wire while talking to his fellow crew members. Justice Department Photo.

Although "Uncle Sam" had contended that eight men were involved in the Balmoral job, only seven were indicted. The eighth person turned out to be Paul "Peanuts" Panczko, a member of the legendary Panczko Clan. Panczko, a career criminal, had turned government informant and in 1985 began wearing a wire, secretly tape recording conversations with underworld associates.

One of those who talked out of school to Panczko was defendant "Duke" Basile. When Basile realized that Panczko had tape recorded him on a number of occasions he, like Saul on the road to Damascus, saw "the light." Basile then got into the act and started wearing a wire himself. Before his undercover role was revealed "Duke" estimated that had he taped some one hundred and eighty conversations.

Perhaps the most bizarre twist of the case came during the 1989 trial when Gerald "Bootsie" Ciancio testified for the prosecution under a grant of immunity. Ciancio was still a defendant but was to be tried separately. He told a Federal Court jury that DiCaro forced him at gunpoint to accompany the burglary crew to the racetrack. Sitting in the witness stand in the courtroom of Judge Harry Leinenweber Ciancio testified:

"He (DiCaro) pulled out a gun and said 'don't worry about a thing. You go and turn this thing (alarm) down and you can go home.'" According to Ciancio he did as he was told and turned off the burglar alarm...

When asked by prosecutors who else was involved in the job, Ciancio's memory began to get a little hazy. He testified that he saw some other people but didn't know who they were. Ciancio, as we mentioned earlier, was scheduled to be tried separately. But the charges were dropped after he testified against DiCaro.

Basile and Panczko were the key witnesses for the government at the trial. They named names on the witness stand, tying some of the defendants to the Balmoral job. Perhaps more effective from the prosecution standpoint were the taped conversations that were played in open court.

In one 1988 conversation which took place at a Chicago restaurant, Gurgone implicated himself in the Balmoral heist, while he and Basile dined on grilled cheese and hamburger sandwiches that were washed down with chocolate milkshakes.

Panczko, meanwhile, had engaged in a number of chats with Thomas Harty. At the time of the attempted heist Harty, was sixty two, the oldest member of the gang. For that matter, nobody in the crew could have been labeled a spring chicken.

The unsuspecting Harty was suffering from foot in mouth disease when he talked to Panczko. Not only did he reminisce about Balmoral but he also, authorities said, implicated himself in two currency exchange robberies.

The tapes pretty much nailed the defendants to the cross. The jury returned guilty verdicts against four of the five who were on trial.

Paul DiCaro, described by assistant U.S. Attorney John Scully as one of the "top commercial thieves" in Chicago, received a six year sentence. The six year hitch wasn't to take effect until 1996 when DiCaro was scheduled to be released from a lengthy jail term he was already serving on theft and robbery charges. The theft and robbery incident occurred before the Balmoral case.

Defendant Gurgone, called a "Dr. Jekyl and Mr. Hyde," by Judge Leinenweber was also handed a six year term.

Leinenweber dropped the shoe on defendant Lesczynski. "Wally the Polack," who was fifty nine at the time of sentencing, drew a ten year jail term. Prosecutors had asked for even a longer jail term, describing Lesczynski as a "very, very dangerous man."

Wheelman Harty, the senior citizen of the group, ended up with three years. The sixty-three-year-old Harty would have gotten a stiffer sentence, the Judge explained, if he were a younger man.

Although Basile was sentenced to ten years, he was given a new identity and reportedly went into the Federal witness protection program.

As for Panczko, he was given a reduced sentence and soon surfaced again. "Peanuts" married former Chicago madam, Dolly Fisher and we presume will live happily ever after. As we said at the outset, the Balmoral caper had a happy ending.

THE STRANGE CASE OF DR. JAMES MIDDLETON

I used to see him every day at the 1986 trial of two Cook County Sheriff's Officers who were being tried on bribery charges.

The tall distinguished looking man, always dressed in a business suit, was not a journalist covering the case for a newspaper or TV station. He was not a free lance writer doing a piece for a magazine. He was not a member of the court buffs, a group of mostly retired men and women who are found each day in courtrooms at the Dirksen Federal Building. And he was not a friend or relative of the defendants.

Yet this stern looking middle aged man took notes just like a reporter would. It turned out that the spectator in the courtroom was Dr. James Middleton who had been dubbed by the media in the early 1970s as the "Sex Doctor."

Middleton's daily pilgrimages to the courtroom got under the skin of one of the defendants, Sgt. Bruce Frasch. One day, during a break in the proceedings Frasch approached Middleton and said something to him. It was obvious to onlookers that Frasch was agitated and had not stopped by to wish the doctor a cheerful good morning. Middleton told me later that Frasch had "cussed him out." Did the two men have a grudge against each other? Not according to Middleton who said he had never met Frasch before. And Frasch never explained, at least to any reporters, at to why he was sore at Middleton.

When the two cops were convicted in what was known as the Operation Safebet case, Middleton called it "a form of justice." Middleton contended he had been framed by Sheriff's Policemen.

Middleton claimed vice officers tried to shake him down just like Frasch and his fellow defendant had done to bookmakers and prostitutes.

Middleton's problems with the Cook County Sheriff's Department stemmed from a December, 1970 raid at his suburban Des Plaines medical offices. According to Middleton, a general practitioner, the cops kept him handcuffed to a door for more than four hours while they looked for evidence. The police said they went to Middleton's offices after several of the doctor's female patients complained that he had drugged them and sexually assaulted them.

The way Middleton tells it one of the raiding officers said he would let the doctor "off the hook" if he would come up with sixty thousand dollars. Middleton claims when he said no to the alleged bribe offer he was placed under arrest and charged with drugging and sexually assaulting one of his female patients.

It was not the first time that Middleton had run a foul of the law. In 1961 while practicing medicine in the St. Louis, Missouri area he was a defendant in a similar case. He was accused of drugging and raping one of his female patients. Although Middleton was acquitted, Missouri medical authorities revoked his license. Middleton then moved to Illinois where he hung up his shingle in the Chicago area.

But Middleton's legal woes in Illinois weren't confined to the sexual assault case. Federal authorities got into the act and charged the besieged M.D. with possession of explosives. It seems the night the lawmen visited Middleton's Des Plaines offices, they found a quantity of gunpowder and what was described by investigators as a bomb cache. Police said they recovered blasting caps, detonators, and several pipe bombs. Middleton conceded he had gunpowder and some other explosive material in his offices. But Middleton described the seized objects as pyrotechnics. He claimed he was using the material in research. The doctor said he was trying to develop flares for signaling devices that he hoped to market.

Soon the media was getting it's money's worth out of the Middleton story. Middleton was called the "Sex Case Medic" or the

"Sex Doctor." Readers were led to believe that lurid details of the assault case would come out at the trial. Then more information about Middleton hit the fan.

It occurred at his Federal trial when Middleton took the stand in the case where he was accused of illegal possession of explosives. Testifying in his own behalf, Middleton told Judge James Parsons that he had worked for the Central Intelligence Agency from 1951 to 1953. Middleton wouldn't elaborate on what he did for the super secret spy agency, saying he was not at liberty to divulge such information. Middleton was telling the truth. Washington sources confirmed that Middleton, prior to becoming a doctor, had been with the CIA for two years.

Not long ago Middleton told me he had served in the operations division working overseas, in Europe, in a clandestine capacity. But Middleton said his cover was blown by Kim Philby, the former British secret intelligence agent, who was actually a Soviet mole. Philby for years had been feeding the Russians top secret Allied intelligence information. Middleton claimed Philby pretty much put the kibosh on his role as a secret operative, so he resigned from the CIA. That's when Middleton said he went back to the states where he went to medical school, getting his M.D. from St. Louis University.

Middleton's CIA ties didn't keep him out of a Federal hoosegow. Judge Parsons, in a bench trial, found the doctor guilty of possessing explosives. Middleton ended up serving fourteen months at the Federal correctional facility at Sandstone, Minnesota. But we're getting ahead of our story. The trial that got the headlines was the state case where Middleton was charged with deviate sexual assault.

The state's case against Middleton was based on the complaint of a twenty-four-year-old housewife and part time model from suburban Carpentersville. Middleton claimed the woman's modeling career was confined to doing lingerie shows before ogling businessmen at a suburban bar and restaurant.

But the woman's modeling career was not an issue at the trial. Police said other female patients had complained about Middleton's bedside manner. The women alleged that Middleton had drugged them and then sexually assaulted them. But the only criminal charge against Middleton was based on the allegations of the states star witness, the former model. She testified that she had visited Middleton's office ten times between December of 1969 and February of 1970. The woman told a criminal court jury of eight men and four women that on February 7th Middleton injected her with a drug that made her shake and shiver, leaving her with no muscular control. Then about a half an hour after being injected with the drug, the witness testified, Middleton came back to the examining room and assaulted her as she lay on a table.

Middleton had his day in court too. Middleton took the stand denying that he had drugged or assaulted the ex-model. And Middleton's lawyers contended the woman's motive in making the criminal complaint against their client was to bolster a one point two million dollar civil suit she had filed earlier against the doctor.

Four other former women patients also took the stand for the state. They too said they had been drugged. They testified that the drugs had left them in a stupor and that they had left the examining room without any idea of what had occurred.

So the jury heard conflicting testimony. They opted not to believe Middleton. After fourteen and a half hours of deliberation, the jury found Middleton guilty of deviate sexual assault. Middleton was not jailed immediately. He remained free on appeal bond enabling him to prepare for the civil case. By this time, 1976, the doctor, his license revoked, was indigent. He acted as his own attorney in the civil trial. Again, as in the criminal case, the jury believed the former patient. The ex-model won an eighty thousand dollar judgment. But Middleton, as of late 1996, said he had not paid a penny to the ex-model. Middleton said he had no funds.

Long before the civil case was resolved, the Middleton scenario took another strange twist. That happened on June 13, 1972, four months after Middleton was convicted. That was the day Judge Robert Downing denied Middleton's motion for a new trial. There was nothing unusual about that. But at the same hearing Middleton accused prosecutor James Kavanaugh of calling him at home on the night of February 24, 1972. That's the same day Middleton was sentenced to five to ten years in prison. According to Middleton, Kavanaugh told him perjured testimony had been used against the doctor.

Dr. James Middleton was called the "Sex Doxtor" by the media. He claims he was framed by Sheriff's Police.

Kavanaugh had indeed called Middleton that night. Kavanaugh told Judge Downing: "I called him (Middleton) up that night because I couldn't get it out of my mind. I had some drinks, I couldn't get it out of my mind that he would take some action against my wife and children."

Judge Downing: "When you called him what was the first thing you said?"

Kavanaugh: "That I'm a professional and I only prosecuted you (Middleton) because I'm a prosecutor. I hope you don't have any ill feelings toward me."

Kavanaugh also testified that he asked Middleton if he thought that he (Kavanaugh) had knowingly been involved in any conspiracy against him. Kavanaugh told the Judge that Middleton replied that he did not think so.

Judge Downing ruled that there had been no evidence of perjured testimony or any evidence of a conspiracy against Middleton. Downing though chastised Kavanaugh for making such a phone call to a defendant calling it "improper and unprofessional."

The tongue lashing of an assistant States Attorney did Middleton little good. The doctor was sent off to jail. He spent four years in the Illinois prison system, most of it at a minimum security facility. It wasn't hard time compared to the big houses at Stateville and Pontiac but prison is still prison.

Despite Middleton's rash of troubles his wife, Margaret, an ex-Navy WAVE, stayed with her husband through thick and thin. She became the breadwinner in the family and still is as of this writing.

Middleton continues to insist he was framed. You'll see him sometimes at trials or hearings where he believes the defendant was set up or framed. In those instances, Middleton says, he can identify himself with the defendant's plight. Although the courts have affirmed Middleton's guilt, the onetime CIA operative will go to his grave claiming he got a raw deal.

You may see Middleton sitting among the spectators at a criminal case. He's a tall man, wears spectacles, and has aged gracefully. He's seventy two years old now, having been born in 1926. Some of the court buffs call him the "avenger." It's a moniker Middleton seems to like.

JOHN DEJOHN

Nothing ever went right for him. "Lady luck" may have blessed some of his Mobster pals but she turned her back on John DeJohn. DeJohn ended up with nothing but an arrest record that dated back some thirty years, a suit of prison denims to keep him warm, and finally eight bullet holes in his fifty-one-year-old body.

DeJohn reminded you of a bit player in an old George Raft movie, a tough talking small time hood who lived in the shadow of the underworld and his tough talking buddies.

John DeJohn first contacted me in 1979 when he was being held at the Metropolitan Correctional Center in downtown Chicago. He was being held there awaiting one of his numerous court appearances. DeJohn had grown disenchanted with some of his Mob associates and wanted to put some heat on them. He supplied me with an organizational chart, listing the Capos and soldiers of a North Side street crew. DeJohn also talked to the FBI in Chicago giving them the same information. Frankly, there was nothing fresh or new in his material. It was old stuff. It had been reported on before.

It seemed DeJohn almost had a death wish. When we talked to him at the MCC he seemed resigned to a violent end. He seemed obsessed about weapons and what damage they could do. DeJohn didn't beat around the bush about his future plans: "I like guns. I like to hurt people who do me wrong because I've been hurt so much. I really don't care if I live or die."

In 1981, shortly after he was paroled from a Federal penitentiary on a stolen securities conviction DeJohn did indeed meet a violent end.

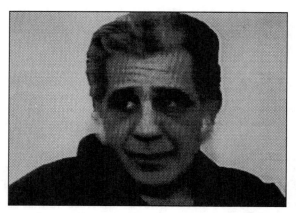

John DeJohn, small-time hood. Ended-up with eight bullets in his body — murdered in gangland style.

DeJohn called me several days before he was murdered. He was staying at a small hotel off of Rush Street, he said. He wanted to talk to me but felt he had to watch his step. John was concerned that if he was seen talking to a reporter, it could be curtains for him.

The next thing I heard about DeJohn was that his bullet riddled body had been dumped in an alley on the Northwest Side. John had been shot in the chest, back, and head. Detectives said DeJohn had been lured to his death by the promise of a big score. The alleged score was a set up. DeJohn had been taken for a one way ride. Although police said they couldn't prove who killed DeJohn they felt they knew why he had been slain. Veteran Area Five detective Jack Leonard put it this way: "John DeJohn talked too much. He would just talk to too many people about too many things, and he really had no substantial information. He just knew a lot of names."

John DeJohn never made the big score that he always dreamed about. Instead his life revolved around a bunch of "pooch" crimes such as stealing cars and passing bad checks.

While John DeJohn's life was on a toboggan slide his two brothers had done well. One went to law school and became an attorney in Chicago. The other a successful banker.

Ironically DeJohn's father, Nicholas, a longtime Chicago gambling boss, was also slain in gangland style. The elder DeJohn was murdered in San Francisco in 1947 where he had gone to escape a wave of gangland assassinations in Chicago.

The murder of his father, the subsequent death of his mother and a divorce seemed to have unhinged John DeJohn. The combination of the three may have pushed DeJohn into his role as a small time hoodlum.

The 1947 murder of Nicholas DeJohn was never solved and the sordid demise of John DeJohn probably won't be either.

CHAPTER TEN

Down and Out

A WALK ON THE WILD SIDE

I once knew a gentleman who I thought, at the time, had one of the best jobs in the world. He worked for the Miller Brewing Company of Milwaukee. No, he wasn't a high ranking executive with a big salary, stock options, a country club membership, and other fringe benefits. He was a good will man for Miller and his job was to visit taverns, buy drinks for the house, and look like he was having a good time as he pushed what was then called Miller High Life.

I was about twenty years old when I met the man and I was pretty impressionable. Frankly, I envied the man. Not only did he get all the free beer he wanted but he got paid for drinking it.

A couple of years later I ran into the Miller goodwill man again. He told me he had quit his job with the brewery. I was stunned that anybody would pull out of that kind of deal but the onetime Miller man said he was heading for an early grave if he didn't bail out. He explained that, as a good will man, he had to drink with the customers when he ordered a round. Otherwise, he said, it would appear that he didn't like the product he was promoting.

My friend said he would visit up to seven or eight taverns a day, mostly of the neighborhood variety. In each place he would normally have a couple of beers before shoving off to another gin mill.

The former goodwill man told me that he had a perpetual glow on and was putting on too much weight. He complained that his only relief from talking to slightly inebriated patrons came when he made frequent trips to the tavern's mens room. The ex-Miller man said he was concerned that he was becoming an alcoholic so he got out, as he put it, "while the going was good."

Liquor investigator Jim Hackleman field tests
suspected bottle in a Chicago tavern.

I thought my old friend had visited more taverns than anyone else on this planet until I met two Chicagoans, Jim Hackleman and Terry Selivon. Those two guys have been to more bars than any two fisted drinker I've ever met. You see, Hackleman and Selivon were agents with the Illinois Liquor Control Commission. Their task was to visit taverns in the Chicago area to make sure that bartenders and owners were playing according to "Hoyle."

It was always one of my favorite assignments to accompany Commission agents as they went about their business. They would make the rounds looking for a variety of violations. Those violations ranged the gamut from re-filling top brands with cheaper stock to having contaminated booze on the premises.

Hackleman and Selivon's tools of the trade were test tubes and other devices geared to determine if liquor was being tampered with at a citizen's favorite watering hole.

At times those visits by the agents were something of a walk on the wild side, particularly when the twosome checked out bars on Madison Street and Wilson Avenue, two of the least affluent areas in the City of Chicago.

But don't get the idea that violations were only found in skid row dumps or mama and papa neighborhood joints. The agents said that high class cocktail lounges were also sometimes involved in some form of hanky panky.

Liquor investigators say that high priced brands of liquor, the so-called top shelf stuff, are often the targets of refilling. This is a practice known as watering down liquor. It doesn't mean partially filling a bottle of good booze with water. Instead, the unscrupulous bartender or owner will take a cheaper brand and pour it's contents into a half filled or three quarters filled bottle of expensive whiskey, gin, or vodka.

Agents say old labels, worn strip stamps, or bottles filled too high are often indications that liquor has been tampered with. When agents suspect tampering they will take out test tubes, chemicals, other paraphernalia and conduct a field test in the bar. If the field test indicates tampering, the agents will take the suspected bottles to a state lab for a more thorough analysis.

Irate customers suspicious that their drinks have been watered down sometimes write letters to the commission relaying their concerns. Another source of information comes from disgruntled employees who will write or call the commission making allegations of wrongdoing. The Liquor Control Commission, though, says most bar patrons can't tell if their liquor has been watered down.

In some obvious cases, such as contaminated bottles of liquor, swarming with insects known as fruit flies, the agents don't bother with a field test. The bottles are removed from the shelves and taken to the lab. We saw a number of instances of this when we were out on patrol with Hackleman, Selivon, and some of their colleagues.

The watering holes where we found evidence of fruit flies were not the kind of spots where the Perrier crowd would gather. At one bar where the agents saw obvious instances of contamination, you didn't need a lab test to confirm that insects were in the bottle. You could actually see the fruit flies swirling around.

That didn't surprise Frank, the popular mixologist on duty. He pointed to his customers and told me "we get plenty of flies in here, bar flies that is." That brought loud guffaws from some of the human bar flies sitting on nearby stools.

Bar patron downs a shot of whiskey. Fruit flies were drowned in the whiskey, but that didn't bother the patron.

Incidentally most of the places we visited with Liquor Commission agents had a good number of patrons seated at the bar even though our stops came around mid-morning or even earlier. Some of the early birds appeared to need a shot and a beer to give them a steady hand before venturing outside.

At another bar, a place where many in the thirsty crowd looked like they were a step away from skid row, more flies were found in bottles. That didn't phase one middle aged customer who called himself John. John didn't beat around the bush when it came to bugs in bottles. With a straight face John rattled on: "all my life I've been around whiskey and wine. We eat so many bugs and dirt in our lifetime that it doesn't bother me at all."

After his frank commentary John had the bartender pour him a two ounce shot of whiskey from the bottle filled with floating fruit flies. "Watch me now, I drank my shot. It was bottoms up." With that the grinning John turned toward our camera and said "I ate all my bugs. Boy they are good. You know, I get bugged when I drink, hah, hah."

While investigators and John did their stuff, patrons continued to enjoy their morning bracers. After all, when you can get a shot of Jim Beam for only forty cents and genial companions to imbibe with, it's a temptation to have more than one for the road.

Hackleman and Selivon had a standard operating procedure when checking out a tavern. They would first look over the stock and field test any suspicious bottle for infractions. If the field test indicates there is a problem the bottles are confiscated and taken to the state lab on Chicago's West Side. If the lab tests prove negative the confiscated bottles are returned to the tavern.

Sometimes the street hardened agents are surprised with what they find. On one occasion, in our presence, agents field tested a bottle of wine that had tasted funny. It turned out the "wine" apparently contained no alcohol content at all.

If chemical tests at the lab confirm the agents suspicions, the Liquor Commission can take action. At the time we did our "walks on the wild side" in the late 1970s and mid 80s penalties could range from a four day to a thirty day suspension. If there were repeat incidents, the offending tavern could lose it's license.

Through the years we followed liquor control commission agents making their rounds at least five times. I could never understand why the other TV stations in Chicago never followed suit. If they did, I don't remember it. It was such a great TV story, good pictures, usually a great dialogue. And last but not least it provided a public service. It was both interesting and informative.

Attention assignment editors! If you are looking for a story on a lean news day, you could do a lot worse than follow guys like Jim Hackleman and Terry Selivon as they take a "walk on the wild side." Your viewers will love it.

THE KING OF THE PANHANDLERS

Most every noontime you'd find Floyd Albright plying his trade at the corner of Rush and Illinois streets on Chicago's near North Side. Albright who was also known as "Frank the Bum" or "Frank Johnson" was a panhandler. In fact, Albright was so successful at mooching coins and bills that Floyd was known on the street as the "The King of the Panhandlers."

The bearded Albright, always garbed in an old maroon stocking cap and a tattered overcoat, had his best luck stationed outside the Corona Cafe, a onetime eatery, frequented by advertising executives, news people, and businessmen. On weekends Albright worked Michigan Avenue hitting on the flocks of tourists who strolled up and down the street.

One mark described Floyd as: "Very discriminating. He didn't hit on everyone." There were others who made a daily contribution for one reason or another. Some considered Albright a good luck charm. Floyd had a few trade secrets. And one of them was not to antagonize possible patrons. Unlike some of the Street people who would utter oaths and curses when a would be contributor walked by stiffing them "The King of the Panhandlers" said he took it in stride:

"There's no need for that. I'd say do you have any spare change? And they'll say yes or no. And I say have a nice day."

Albright told me he worked for the *Chicago Tribune* for fifteen years. According to Floyd, when the paper fired him from his job on the loading dock, he became a vagabond. Albright wouldn't say why the *Trib* gave him his walking papers. Floyd had more than his share of job offers. The chef at the Corona, on more than one occasion, asked Floyd if he wanted to work at the restaurant. Albright said no. A waiter at the Corona said he couldn't fault Floyd for not working. After all, the waiter claimed, Albright was making more money panhandling than he was, waiting on tables.

Floyd Albright, "King of the Panhandlers." Shown here plying his trade on the Near North Side.

Nobody knew how much money Albright made hustling on the street. Floyd said on a good day he could take in as much as fifty dollars. Those are 1980 dollars. In one instance, the veteran panhandler claimed an Akron, Ohio businessman, in town for a convention, handed him a one hundred dollar bill.

"He said to me, 'you look like a fine gentlemen, can you use any money?' I said I'd appreciate that and he gave me a one hundred dollar bill."

Albright would make several trips each day to a nearby currency exchange to swap his silver for paper money. Then it was time for Floyd to have a little fun.

Little was known about Albright's non professional life. He hung out at a couple of taverns spending the day's booty on quarts of beer. Floyd was reluctant to talk about where he was from, if he had any family, and where he lived. He once told me he had a room at a Clark Street flophouse. But when we interviewed the manager of the hotel, the man told us that nobody answering to Albright's description lived there.

Four months after profiling Albright on one of our newscasts "The King of the Panhandlers" was on a slab at the Cook County morgue. No, it wasn't rotgut booze or the elements that had done Frank in. He had been murdered by a nineteen-year-old former mental patient whom Albright had befriended. Police said the killer had slit Albright's throat. Detectives determined the two men had quarreled. Robbery, they said, was not the motive. Police found four one dollar bills and eighty-six cents in Albright's pockets. That was the extent of the "King of the Panhandlers" estate.

The murder scene was a street corner only a couple of blocks from the Corona Restaurant where Floyd toiled daily for handouts. It was a spot, fellow panhandlers said, where Albright would often spend the night with a makeshift cardboard box and battered blanket.

Services for Floyd were held several days later at a North Side funeral home. Albright's relatives were there. They said Floyd didn't have to live the life of a street nomad and could have moved in with them. But they said he preferred the lifestyle of a vagrant.

One of those at the funeral service was John Erickson who had shared many a night on the street with Albright. The death of his pal had hit Erickson hard.

"He never bothered nobody. He never did anything to nobody. The guy was my friend."

Erickson who was visibly moved went on "I'm not over this yet, it's going to going to bother me for a long time."

Others paid tribute to "The King of the Panhandlers" in a different way. A bouquet of flowers, a quart of beer, and Albright's beloved stocking cap had been left at the site where Floyd had been murdered. A very simple memorial but I have a feeling that Floyd would have liked it that way.

TREADMILL TO OBLIVION

In it's heyday, the sprawling Madison Street skid row area had more down and outers than anywhere else in the nation. Chicago's skid row was bigger than L.A.'s Main Street, New York's Bowery, or Minneapolis' Washington Avenue.

It would be difficult to say how many urban nomads lived on the row from the late 1940s to the early 60s. That's the period when the skid row population, estimated at around seven thousand, was at it's peak.

I recall visiting the Street during that period. In the jargon of those days the Street vagabonds were called "bums or winos." Such terms are verboten, of course, in these politically correct times.

The chamber of commerce didn't like it but the row was a must stop for tourists. Tourists and suburbanites alike got cheap thrills, cruising the Street seeing derelicts stumbling along the sidewalk, men passed out in doorways and alleys, "winos" swigging rotgut out of filthy bottles, and Street people urinating in public.

However, not everyone who lived on the Street in that period was a panhandler or a hopeless alcoholic. There were also a number of retirees living on modest pensions. Then there were the legions of unskilled workers trying to catch on as gandy dancers, with the railroad, or as dishwashers or whatever jobs that were available at the many day labor centers that dotted the area.

In the Street's so called "golden era" stories would crop up about big shots who ended up on the row because of their fondness for the sauce. You heard tales about doctors, priests, lawyers, CEO's, and professors who were on a treadmill to oblivion. There was one yarn I could not confirm. The operator of a rescue mission told me that a former governor of West Virginia had ended up on Chicago's skid row. According to our source, the former governor finally straightened himself out and got a job driving a cab.

Although there were some men who lived on the row in that era who did not have a drinking problem, the vast majority who ended up on the Street were there because of their daily bouts with "John Barleycorn."

By the time I started doing stories about Madison Street and it's denizens, the wreckers ball had begun to take it's toll. Urban renewal was going into high gear and many of the flop houses and bars in the neighborhood were being demolished in the name of progress. The character of the Street was also changing. Before, the population of skid row was comprised mostly of older white men. By the late 1960s it was a common sight to see men in their twenties and thirties standing in line, with their older colleagues, in front of rescue missions waiting to be fed.

By the late 1970s the majority of Street people were black. And by the mid 80s it was not unusual to see a woman panhandler trying to put the mooch on a mark. But there were those who got off that treadmill to oblivion to live a productive life.

One of them was Harold Downing who I profiled in a 1990 piece. Downing spent seventeen years on the row and authored a book, "Six Thousand Days and Nights on Chicago's Skid Row." The book detailed his Madison Street experiences.

Downing was down and out from 1950 until 1967. He said he drank after shave lotion and canned heat to get his kicks. Downing told me that the turning point in his life came after he was found passed out in a bottle strewn room of a flop house. He was treated at Cook County Hospital and then released. He ended up in a small room of a run down hotel. It was there, Downing said, that he asked God for help:

"I asked God to show me that he was here and I opened the window in that little room and a breeze was coming in moving the curtains. I couldn't see the breeze but it was there."

Downing interpreted that as a message from God. Harold says he has been sober ever since. The last I heard about Downing was that he was working as a maintenance man at a church in suburban Oak Brook.

Harold Downing would hardly recognize the street from the days he drifted aimlessly, trying to cadge drinks from other homeless men. The McCoy Hotel, a Downing hangout, was bulldozed to make way for a commercial building.

Death knell for the Starr Hotel. A wrecker's ball destroys the "Waldorf-Astoria" of skid row.

The wreckers ball also claimed the seven story Starr Hotel, "the Waldorf Astoria of Madison Street." It never got five stars in the Mobil travel guide, but it's rooms, even with the chicken wire ceilings were always a notch above the urine reeked flop houses that once were so numerous in the neighborhood.

Although it lacked the amenities of the Ritz-Carlton the Starr aimed to please. The hotel's fly paper, I might add, always caught it's share of insects. And like the plush hotels on North Michigan Avenue, the Starr had a number of newsworthy lodgers. Mass murderer Richard Speck flopped in room 567 back in 1966 shortly after he had killed eight student nurses.

At one time as many as three hundred residents, paying as much as one dollar and seventy five cents a night, stayed at the

Starr. They were mostly senior citizens living on Social Security. But the occupancy rate dropped as the Street population eventually declined. The city of Chicago acquired the hotel for demolition under urban renewal. By 1982 the Starr was doomed.

That meant men like Charley Hayes, who had lived on the Street since 1945, had to look for new lodging. For Hayes, a kindly elderly man with a paunch, the Starr was his home. Cost wise Hayes felt he couldn't beat the Starr. As he described it, his options were limited:

"You can't find a place this cheap anywhere else."

Hayes' plight was similar to others at the Starr. They couldn't afford to pay the rent at the second rate hotels that were located on the fringe of the loop. Unless Hayes could find space at one of the few skid row flop houses, that were fast disappearing from the scene, he would have no choice but to seek shelter at a rescue mission. There Hayes would have little privacy, sleeping in a dormitory with as many as seventy five men. And that probably would only be a stop gap measure since only a few mission residents are able to stay on as permanent guests.

The Hayes case was typical of many who were living in single occupancy hotels, known as SROs. The hotels, with Spartan furnishings, catered to welfare and Social Security recipients. But in a ten year period from 1976 to 1986, an estimated seventeen SRO units were lost in Chicago.

You don't have to be a sociologist to see why the number of homeless people has increased in Chicago in recent years. With the SRO's rapidly vanishing, the Street people had nowhere to go. Although some of the hotels were fleabags, they at least offered a roof over an occupant's head and a modicum of privacy.

At one time there seemed some kind of bond between the down and outers. But that changed too. Soon more and more predators found that there were easy pickings on the row. These jackal like predators, known on the Street as "jack rollers," would prey on the weak, sick, and helpless. The "jack rollers" had little difficulty in determining when monthly pension or welfare checks would arrive. They would stalk their victims, like the big cats on the African veldt, waiting for a moment of weakness. Then they would pounce, robbing an old man of his few worldly possessions.

I recall once coming upon a victim of a "jack roller." The man had collapsed on the sidewalk his face was bloodied. When I attempted to help him to his feet, the man lashed out with his cane, apparently believing that I was the guy who had robbed him and put him on the deck. So much for being a good Samaritan!

Unwilling guest is escorted to the "Bum Wagon." Madison Street denizen was taken to the detox center.

But there are those who go the good Samaritan route every day. On one occasion I followed two cops as they cruised the street, in a paddy wagon, looking for derelicts in need of help. In the parlance of the time, the two police officers manned what was then called the "bum wagon." Patrolmen James Smith and Ron McClain who worked out of the Monroe Street district station did not have an enviable assignment.

Their clientele, who reeked with urine and vomit, often did not appreciate the curb service that Smith and McClain provided. Sometimes the arrival of the wagon would disturb a mid day siesta, resulting in a torrent of curses and obscenities. And in a few cases the men would respond to a wagon invitation with kicks and punches.

But Smith a twenty two year department veteran and his younger partner McClain took it all in stride. Actually Smith and McClain were doing the men a favor, particularly those found sprawled on the street, an inviting target for "jack rollers." Obviously the two coppers weren't able to pick up every homeless man who needed attention. You'd have to have a semi trailer to do that.

McClain, the son of a police officer and the nephew of former Detroit Tigers pitching ace, Denny McClain explained to me that their priorities were to find "rowers" who required treatment at the city's detoxification center:

"When we approach them, we look at their eyes to see if they're bloodshot. We can also tell the alcoholic odor on them and if they are slow in movement. We can tell from experience that they need to go into the detox center. If nothing else they will be given a hot meal and get cleaned up. This is the service we try to render to them."

Smith and McClain were realists who knew that their efforts were merely stop gap measures which provided only a temporary roadblock to a street person's downward slide.

Once out of detox the men had little trouble finding run down bars where the wine was cheap and the conversation animated. The best known of Madison Street saloons was Sid's Junction, a tavern only a stone's throw away from the aforementioned Starr Hotel.

To many of it's habitues, Sid's was a home away from home. A place to talk about the good old days or curse the day that "demon rum" dictated their fate.

Sid's like the Starr is gone now. A building housing Social Security offices sits across the street. Three skyscrapers, filled mostly with upwardly mobile professionals, stands a couple of blocks to the east. There are still a few missions, that have been able to escape the wrecker's ball. But they are the only remnants on a street that once attracted thousands of homeless men who were seeking cheap lodging, food and liquor.

There are a few people left who worked the street in it's halcyon days. The most prominent of that vanishing breed is Monsignor Ignatius McDermott or "Father Mac" as he is better known.

*Mscr. Ignatius McDermott. Father "Mac" is known as
"The Skid Row Pastor."*

For more than forty years "Father Mac's" parish has been what cynics have called the flotsam of the street. But "Father Mac" who has been a mainstay for Catholic Charities is not the kind of cleric to throw in the towel when it comes to tending to his flock. He has helped many a parishioner climb out of the gutter to find respectability. And many a hopeless drunk has become sober under "Father Mac's" guidance.

McDermott is no head in the sand do gooder. He knows the street and the people who live on it, like the back of his hand. The Monsignor feels that skid row goes beyond normal street boundaries. As the veteran clergyman puts it: "skid row is not a piece of real estate. It's a state of mind. And I've found as many alcoholics in the penthouse as I've found in the flophouse."

The demise of the old Madison Street area did not eradicate skid row. If anything, the ranks of the homeless are growing. If you don't believe me, walk down North Michigan Avenue or State Street. The odds are someone will ask you for a handout. And before day is done, the chances are that another panhandler will hit you for a piece of change. A generation ago that would only have occurred on Madison Street. But as they say, times are changing.

CHAPTER ELEVEN

The Jocks

HONEYBOY

He was once a World's Champion but we found Johnny Bratton, homeless, roaming the streets in the Old Town and Rush Street areas. Sometimes Johnny would pick up a buck or two mooching off of strangers. His nights were spent sleeping in doorways or in the lobbies of second rate hotels.

It was a far cry from the time that Bratton cruised the southside in a fancy Cadillac with his nickname "Honeyboy" emblazoned on the side. In his heyday Bratton was the welterweight champion of the world. This was the era immediately following World War II, which was considered by some experts as the golden age of boxing in this country.

Bratton was only twenty three years old when he won the 147 pound title by beating Charley Fusari in at the Chicago stadium. That was back in 1951. The local boy had made good, his future as a pugilist seemed bright.

Unfortunately for Johnny, he didn't hold onto the crown for very long. He lost the title later that same year when he was decisioned by the Cuban hawk, Kid Gavilan, a television favorite…

But "Honeyboy," as Bratton was called because he danced so sweet in the ring, was still a headliner, the big paydays continued. He fought in such places as "The Mecca of Mayhem," Madison

Square Garden, the Montreal Forum, the Detroit Olympia, and of course the Chicago stadium.

Johnny "Honeyboy" Bratton, former Welterweight Champ hit the skids after he retired from the ring.

But his grueling bouts with the likes of Gavilan, Ike Williams, Tiger Jones, and other warriors began to take it's toll. Johnny lost a step and was taking shots from fighters who would have had a hard time laying a glove on him in his prime.

It was obvious that Bratton was through when he was kayoed by Del Flanagan in a bout that took place in St. Paul, Minnesota on St. Patrick's day in 1955. A year earlier Bratton had no trouble scoring an easy decision over Flanagan when the two squared off at the Garden. But in the return bout Bratton looked bad. Johnny was being hit at will by Flanagan when the referee mercifully stopped the match. It was Bratton's last fight. He was only twenty seven years old and washed up as a boxer.

Soon there were only fading memories of the glory days, the fancy cars, the cabarets, the women, and the backslappers. Bratton soon drifted out of sight. Then in 1979 we got a call from someone who told us the former champ was down and out. Bratton had become a skid row bum.

But Bratton didn't have to be a homeless panhandler. Johnny's mother told me her son could stay at her comfortable South Side apartment as long as he wanted to. Bratton, though, had no intention of giving up his vagabond lifestyle explaining his decision to remain a drifter with a bizarre reply: "it's freedom, freedom and justice for all. It's like the American flag." It was obvious that Johnny had taken too many punches. He needed help but he stubbornly wouldn't accept any.

There was talk that Bratton and some unsavory companions were rolling tourists in the Rush Street area. He got into trouble with the law. Bratton was arrested on theft charges. Johnny was in no shape to do time in a penitentiary. Instead he ended up at state mental hospital in downstate Manteno. Eventually Johnny got out and was assigned to a halfway house in Chicago. Although many of Bratton's old pals had abandoned him one man, King Solomon, a former fighter looked after him. Solomon kept Johnny away from the street predators that had caused him problems in the past.

For some reason the fight game seems to attract more scam artists and con men than any other sport. Before long imposters purporting to be Bratton began cropping up. As a rule the impostor figures his charade can be worth a few bucks from an unsuspecting mark. And the Bratton imposters conned a few sportswriters who are supposed to be Street smart. In 1986 a Chicago newspaper reported that former welterweight champion Johnny Bratton was living out of shopping bags in Chicago's Lincoln park. It was a fascinating story, except that the real Johnny Bratton was then residing in a halfway house on the far South Side.

There were other Bratton sightings. The *Washington Post* reported in 1991 that Johnny Bratton was hanging out in a New York city gym. The impostor was interviewed by the *Post* and reporters from New York papers and TV stations. The pretender gave his views on the then current crop of pugilists. The story was carried by the wire services. A great yarn but it wasn't true. A lot of scribes had egg on their faces over that one.

Two years later in 1993 the real Johnny Bratton took the ten count. When Johnny Bratton died of heart failure at a suburban hospital his death attracted little attention. There were no headlines to mourn his passing. Once an idol of fistiana in Chicago, Johnny Bratton for all practical purposes had been forgotten.

CAULIFLOWER ALLEY

Before the NFL and the NBA became kingpins on the tube, professional boxing was the biggest draw on television. Managers would wheel and deal to get their boys on the Wednesday night and Friday night fights. Those bouts were seen coast to coast thanks to TV. A TV shot could mean big dough to the boxer and his manager.

Pushing leather was one way for a kid with little education to claw his way out of the ghetto. It was also a way for sharpies, hustlers, and the Mob to make a good buck by exploiting a youngster who had little skills outside the ring.

We've done a number of stories about the fight game and with few exceptions there was one common thread. The champs and near champs, that we profiled, had little to show for their ring efforts but scar tissue and memories.

In 1982 we were on assignment in Miami, Florida waiting for a jury to return a verdict in a racketeering case involving Tony Accardo and some of his associates. Deliberations dragged on for days so we took time out to visit a former boxing champion, Beau Jack.

He was born Sydney Walker but followers of "The Sweet Science" remember him as Beau Jack, the onetime Lightweight Champion of the World. In his heyday, during World War II, Beau Jack was the darling of New York fight fans. He headlined twenty seven cards at Madison Square Garden, a record at the time .In those days Jack pulled more cash customers into the garden than any other fighter. He was excitement personified in the ring. He punched with authority, took a punch real well, and was in perpetual motion once the bell sounded. Boxing writers called Beau Jack one of the most exciting fighters to have ever climbed through the ropes. He wasn't a big man weighing around 135 to 140 pounds in his prime. But fans got their money's worth when Beau Jack put on the padded mittens.

Fast forward to Miami in the early 1980s. The money Beau Jack made in his 112 bout career is gone. Glasses with thick lenses cover the scar tissue around his eyes. Those lethal hands that once rained blows on an opponent with the speed of a gatling gun were now doing a workmanlike job on a pair of shoes. Jack, you see was working as a bootblack at the Doral Hotel in Miami Beach shining shoes in the hotel barber shop.

Jack wouldn't talk about what happened to those big purses he made as champion. He told us there were more important things in life than money. And Jack who was then sixty one years old, recalled about a vow he made to his grandmother to lead a clean life.

"I'm not worrying about the money. If I didn't get one penny, I just want to prove to my grandmother. That's all I worry about."

Beau Jack practices what he preaches. In his spare time Jack can be found at a gym in Miami's ghetto teaching young men to box. When we visited the gym Jack appeared to be a stern taskmaster to his young charges as he put them through their paces. Jack conceded that he would love to see one of his young fighters become a champion. But he said that was not one of his priorities. Jack stressed that his main goal was to take kids off of street corners and give them something to do.

From the time he began fighting four rounders in New England to his days as a boxing instructor at an inner city gym in Miami Beau Jack has done a lot for boxing. Unfortunately the moguls of the fight game, who made a good buck off of Jack, never gave Beau anything in return.

Freddie Dawson was a Chicago lightweight who had to become a globetrotter to make ends meet. Freddie's problem was that he was too good! Managers wouldn't let Freddie in the ring with their boys because they were concerned that Dawson would make their fighters look bad. So Dawson had to make a number of trips to Australia where he kayoed the best the Aussies had to offer.

*Freddie Dawson, boxing's uncrowned champion. He never
got a fair shake from the powers that be.*

Because several 135 pound titleholders refused to climb in the
ring with Dawson, Freddie was called the "uncrowned champion."

Dawson though, in 1949, finally got a shot at the championship. The Mob guys, who had a stranglehold on many of the top
fighters then, bowed to public pressure. Dawson was given the
green light to challenge Ike Williams in Philadelphia. Williams was
handled by Frank "Blinky" Palermo, a well known Philadelphia
Mob figure. The deck was stacked against Dawson. In order to win
he would have had to either knockout Williams or score a lopsided
decision. Freddie failed to do either and lost a close decision to the
champion. Freddie explained to me years later that even if he had
won the fight, the Mob would still have had a nice payday:

"In the event that I had whipped Ike Williams I would have
been getting only forty percent of my money. The rest would have
gone to the people."

Dawson always referred to the crime syndicate as the "people."

Dawson had to retire in the early 1950s because of eye problems brought on by his long ring career. His handlers and greedy
promoters had gotten their lunch hooks into Dawson's purses and
Freddie had little, if any money left, when he hung up the gloves.

But Dawson stayed in the game after he retired. He trained boxers at a gym on Chicago's South Side. Freddie spent long hours stressing fundamentals to his young charges:

"I can show them how to pull a jab, toss a right cross or a left hook. I can teach them to skip rope and do exercises. If they put it all together they can become fighters."

Unfortunately nobody in Dawson's stable made it big money wise. And Freddie went to his grave without ever producing a champion. But it wasn't for lack of effort.

Dawson despite his superior ring skills often boxed for coffee and cake money. And to the day he died Dawson remained embittered about the large purses handed out to present day fighters who couldn't hold a candle to Freddie when he was in his prime:

"I'm fighting a ten rounder with one of the toughest guys in the world getting two hundred and fifty dollars. These guys are getting one hundred thousand dollars, fifty thousand dollars making all this money. I can't understand it, I can't understand it."

Chicagoan Johnny Paychek had the dubious distinction of being a member of Joe Louis' "Bum of the Month Club." In the "Brown Bomber's" prime, Louis took on all comers usually dispatching his opponents with ease. One year, 1941, Louis defended his title eight times. That's almost one title bout a month. Louis barnstormed around the country sending his would be challengers into dreamland. An enterprising sportswriter came up with the "bum of the month" moniker. Although Johnny Paychek was not a great fighter he wasn't a bum by pugilistic standards. Paychek, one of seven children, came out of a Chicago neighborhood where most breadwinners toiled in the nearby stockyards. But Paychek had his sights set on bigger things. He won a golden gloves title and then turned pro. As a professional Paychek posted forty five wins, two losses and two draws. That's a pretty impressive record.

Johnny is best remembered for his 1940 bout at Madison Square Garden with the legendary Louis. Paychek who appeared very nervous as he climbed into the ring, was obviously overmatched. Paychek has never forgotten that night:

Johnny Paycheck. A member of Joe Louis' "Bum of the Month Club" he was kayoed by the "Brown Bomber."

"I knew was I in for a tough fight. Before I knew what had happened the bout was over. I couldn't comprehend that I was fighting for the championship. It just didn't seem real to me."

Paychek was kayoed in the second round by Louis who had hardly worked up a sweat. Ringsiders said it appeared that Paychek was afraid of Louis. If he was, you couldn't blame him. "The Brown Bomber" was one of the most devastating punchers of all time.

Paychek was through after the Louis fight. He had a couple more matches but Johnny didn't have it anymore. Eventually Johnny got a job pushing a broom instead of leather. For twelve years he worked as a custodian at a suburban high school. Then he retired, spending his golden years with his wife, Alice. By the time Johnny had become a senior citizen Paychek had soured on the fight game that had brought him fleeting fame:

"It's too dangerous. The benefits you gain aren't worth the danger you subject yourself to. The punishment, it's damaging."

And then Paychek echoed what so many former fighters have complained about. Where did the purses go?

"The fighters rarely get to keep what they made. They pay an awful price, it's not worth it."

When I told people I was doing a story about Johnny Paychek, they thought I was doing a piece on the country and western singer by the same name. As they say fame is fleeting.

THE GRUNT AND GROANERS

Through the years we've done a number of stories about pro wrestling. Those yarns included profiles of the wrestlers, the fans, and the promoters. In fact, on one occasion, during a ratings period, we did a two part series on the mat game. Judging by viewer response the grunt and groaners had a foothold on a good segment of our audience. Viewers apparently had a lot of fun watching the two pieces that we put on the air.

Any resemblance between professional wrestling and the collegiate variety is strictly coincidental. Although purists may look with disfavor on pro wrestling, the fans who flock to big arenas around the country to see pro matches, could care less.

Speaking of fans, that's a story in itself. We've covered several matches where weapon wielding fans have tried to wreak vengeance on grapplers who had worked over their favorite wrestler.

Cynics may argue that the current breed of matmen would be more at home in the screen actors guild than in the ring. But frankly, the hippodrome antics are needed to attract the fans.

Grappling legends like Frank Gotch, George Hackenschmidt, and other pioneers, who engaged in straight but often marathon matches, would probably be box office flops today. One wag suggested that the 1911 bout between Gotch, an Iowa farm boy, and Hackenschmidt, "The Russian Lion," was one of the last shooting matches to have taken place. A shooting match is jargon for a legitimate bout. Gotch won that match which was held at Comiskey park in Chicago.

Promoters soon realized that to consistently draw fans they had to come up with gimmicks. Straight or so-called scientific wrestling won't make the turnstiles click. And click they have done in Chicago and many other cities.

In 1961, thirty eight thousand fans, an all time record, saw Buddy Rogers dethrone Pat O'Connor in an outdoor card at Comiskey park. The bout got plenty of pre-fight hype and the fans bought it hook, line, and sinker.

Despite the circus like atmosphere, the pro grapplers earn their money. They take their share of physical abuse from both opponents and fans alike. Many of the professional matmen are former college wrestlers or former pro football players. Others get on the mat circuit via the body building route.

Although the matches may not be the "real McCoy," wrestlers have got to know how to fall properly, how to pull a punch, and how to choreograph a pier six brawl. It's not that easy to come out unscathed. Broken bones, back injuries, and getting teeth knocked out all come with the turf. As "Moose" Cholak can attest to.

Cholak was a Chicago favorite for years with his famous El Squasho submission hold. "Moose" was a mat villain in his younger days but then Cholak saw the error of his ways and became a good guy.

We had a good chat with "Moose" one night back in 1980 when he was tending bar at his family's tavern on the far South Side. Cholak told us that he had more than his share of bruises:

"When I first started wrestling, I was hurt all the time, I busted my shoulder, I dislocated my pelvis, I busted my hip, I had knee injuries, it's a tough business."

Lady wrestlers or "mat maidens," as they were called years ago, also get hurt. One former gal grappler who was billed as "Ginny Gallant," said it wasn't worth getting banged up:

"I had both my feet broken. I injured my back and I had a broken nose. I felt, after all these injuries and after some nagging from my boy friend, it was time to quit."

Other wrestlers we have interviewed have similar tales to tell. But many, particularly the headliners, stay in the game because of the money.

Major pro wrestling matches in Chicago are now held at either the Rosemont Horizon or the University of Illinois Pavilion. They are modern arenas equipped with many amenities. But they seem sterile and bland for the mat sport.

They are a far cry from the musty old International Amphitheater on Chicago's South Side where bouts were held regularly in pro wrestling's halcyon days. There fans, most always raucous and sometimes violent, would jam the rafters. To protect the wrestlers, specifically the villains, a phalanx of security men would escort the grapplers to and from the dressing room. But even with such protection there would be incidents.

I remember one night when a fan, brandishing a knife, tried to attack wrestler Ernie Ladd. Then there was the night, a fan sitting in the balcony of the Amphitheater, became enraged when the referee failed to disqualify Nick Bockwinkle who was acting in a dastardly fashion. The irate fan, pulled out a hand gun and began firing wildly. But instead of hitting his target, either the referee or Bockwinkle, a young ringsider was shot. Fortunately, the young man who had been shot recovered from his wounds. The gunman was never apprehended.

Some of the fans who attended matches at the Amphitheater believed they were seeing the real thing. So it was easy to understand why, sometimes, they would get out of hand.

It's a great gimmick to strut around as a goose-stepping Nazi or a half crazed ape-like creature. But when a wrestler goes that route, and works over the good guy or "baby face," the fans can get ugly. The fans seek revenge and want to see the villain take his lumps. It's a great way to sell tickets but promoters can't cry in their beer if ringsiders go bonkers. Sometimes the violence inside the squared circle triggers beefs outside the ring. I once observed two female spectators tossing punches at ringside. They were thrown out by security guards. While it lasted, it was the best fight of the night.

Watching the spectators can be a show in itself. Each time I did a wrestling story I made a point to talk to the fans. I remember interviewing one glassy eyed guy who was getting his "rocks off" as two behemoths slugged it out in the ring.

"I like the excitement, I like the excitement," he told me. Eyes glazed, he went on, "They hit each other, they strike each other. "'

Another man with bloodshot eyes, "I like to see dirty 'rassling."

A toothless woman who hated the villains but liked the clean wrestlers, "They're such fine young men, they're so wholesome."

A middle aged woman wearing a big hat, complained about the referee, "This mother fucker is no good, I want good referees."

When I worked at Channel 13 in Rockford, in the early 1960s, the station broadcast matches that had been filmed earlier at the Amphitheater or Marigold Gardens in Chicago. We would get numerous phone calls from viewers, who were enraged because they felt that the referees would seldom penalize wrestlers who were "dirty."

At first I would tell these concerned callers that the matches weren't on the square and that the ring officials were part of the act. That failed to satisfy the vast majority of the callers who would scream into the phone "You can't tell me that wasn't real blood, etc., etc."

Finally I got wise and started expressing concern about incompetent officiating. I suggested that if they wanted justice done, they should write a letter to Joe Triner, the then head of the Illinois State Athletic Commission.

Apparently many of these fans did just that! But Triner didn't appreciate the fan mail. He wrote the station, stating he was "sick and tired" of receiving mail and phone calls from Rockford area residents who were upset about the officiating. Triner and his fellow commissioners may have been unhappy about the deluge of mail but, at least, we got the monkey off of our backs.

One of the reasons I enjoyed doing an occasional story about pro wrestling was because of the many colorful characters you'd encounter. And one of the most colorful, was promoter Bob Luce.

Luce, a drum-beater of the old school, was the man mainly responsible for the resurgence of pro wrestling in Chicago in the

1970s. Luce, by the way, wasn't the only member of his family active in the mat game. His blonde wife wrestled under the name of Sharon Glass.

Luce wrote stories for the "National Tattler" magazine before turning his attention to the ring. Bob could really hype a card, making it appear that his feature match would be the biggest grudge fight since Cain met Abel.

Bob did his own spots on TV and along with some of his wrestlers would also do the spieling for the sponsors who bought time on the shows packaged by Luce.

Luce's cards at the Amphitheater would draw between eight thousand and ten thousand fans (ten was capacity). He didn't gouge the customers and his shows were reasonably priced. That may have accounted for the big houses that he would get.

In the summer, Luce would stage outdoor extravaganzas at local ballparks. Those affairs would usually feature battle royals or cage matches. One, I recall was billed as the "Super Bowl" of wrestling.

Luce and his partner, former wrestler, Vern Gagne, eventually lost their stranglehold on the Chicago wrestling scene when the World Wrestling Federation came to town. The WWF brought in a new stable of grapplers, including the popular Hulk Hogan.

The WWF marketed a new breed of wrestling entertainment and the public apparently bought it. For a time in the WWF era, pro wrestling lost it's blue collar image. It became an in thing for yuppies, celebrities, and even rock and roll stars. They sometimes got involved in the pre match hoopla.

Pro wrestling still does well on cable, but the yuppie and celebrity crowd that made the pro mat sport trendy in the mid 80s have lost interest and have moved on to greener pastures.

However, the mat game will always have a fan base. New heroes will come along to replace aging super stars and new villains will come along to take the place of long time "bad guys" who have worn out their welcome.

That brings us to a story about two mat villains who wore out their welcome in Waukesha, Wisconsin and ended up in the slammer. The two matmen who played the heel role outside the ring were Ken Patera, a onetime Olympic weight lifter, and his tag team partner, Masanori Saito, AKA "Mr. Torture." The two ring veterans suffered a Big Mac attack following a bout in nearby Watertown, Wisconsin.

The two wrestlers were staying at the Waukesha Holiday Inn. But by the time they got back to the motel, the motel restaurant was closed. So the two hungry grapplers walked over to a McDonald's where people were still eating. Patera and Mr. Saito though, were told they couldn't be served becuase the restaurant was closing.

The two mat villains spotted a tray of hamburgers that were slated to be thrown out. When they asked an employee if they could buy the burgers, destined for disposal, they were told the hamburgers were not for sale. The McDonald's employee, with Patera and Mr. Saito looking on, reportedly dumped the hamburgers into a waste receptacle.

That, according to authorities, enraged the wrestlers. Moments later somebody threw, what was described as a thirty pound rock or boulder through a window of the restaurant.

Soon the cops arrived on the scene and they traced the wrestlers, to their room at the Holiday Inn. What followed was a battle royal that turned into a mis-match.

When the dust of battle had cleared, one police officer suffered a concussion and a broken leg. Another officer, a female, had her skull fractured and seven teeth knocked out. According to the police report, a third officer had part of his ear bitten off.

Eventually reinforcements were called to the motel. But investigators said it wasn't until one of the deputies drew his revolver that an armistice was declared.

In 1985 Patera and Mr. Saito, facing counts of battery and other charges, had their day in court. In Wisconsin you can shoot film or tape in courtrooms. So it wasn't hard to convince management that a trip to Waukesha would be well worth it.

Patera told me outside the courtroom that he expected to be vindicated. He denied that he threw any rock at a McDonald's window. Mr. Saito, a former Sumo wrestler from Japan, didn't speak English. He merely grunted to me which I interpreted as a no comment.

Patera who was ranked by a wrestling magazine as one of the ten most hated grapplers in the game said the trial was hurting him, where it hurt most, in the pocketbook. Patera said he had big expenses like everyone else:

"It's expensive, it's very costly. Money I can't afford to lose by missing shows on the road. I've got lawyers fees, court costs. Everyone thinks I'm a millionaire which I'm not. I'm a working stiff trying to make a buck like everyone else."

The blond haired Patera's hopes that he and his tag team partner would be vindicated were dashed. The jury didn't buy Patera's story. And neither did the Judge who in sentencing the two gargantuan matmen, likened the one sided motel fight to the "holocaust."

Patera and Mr. Saito were both sentenced to two year prison terms. Mr. Saito did his time washing dishes at a minimum security camp in northern Wisconsin. He reportedly kept in shape by working out up to four hours a day in the camp's weight room.

Patera also did well in jail. He worked on his college degree in physical education through a correspondence course from Brigham Young University. A number of visitors from the ranks of the pro wrestling fraternity would stop at the prison camp near St. Croix, Wisconsin to chat with Patera.

Both men returned to the mat wars following their release from prison.

Although Patera described himself as a "working stiff," grappling headliners are well compensated for their ring efforts. That's one major reason why places like the American Wrestling School have continued to operate through the years.

The walls of the American Wrestling School weren't covered with ivy and the campus was a small third floor room in an aging office building across the street from the Aragon Ballroom, right in the heart of Chicago's Uptown neighborhood.

The students boned up on the works of the Strangler and the Crusher, rather than on Plato and Aristotle. Entry level classes included the full nelson, the hammerlock, and the toe hold. When students graduated they were apt to be sporting a cauliflower ear, instead of a sheepskin.

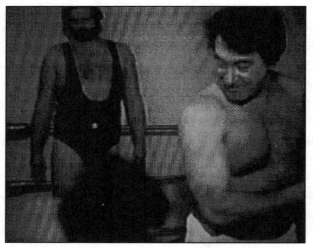

Bob Sabre was known as George Ringo, "The Wrestling Beatle"
in his younger years. Bob later ran a wrestling school in Chicago.

The "professors" at the school were Bob Sabre and a onetime Sabre protege, Kevin Clayton. Sabre had a full-time job as a shipping expediter for a suburban radio supply firm. But a couple of nights a week, he and his partner Clayton would don wrestling togs and teach aspiring novices the tricks of the trade of the grappling profession.

Sabre once toiled under the nom de guerre of George Ringo, the "Wrestling Beatle." That was in the mid 1960s during the height of Beatlemania. Bob made some pretty good money from that gimmick. But when we talked to him in the early 80s Sabre was no longer proud of his Beatle masquerade:

"I'm embarrassed to even talk about that one. Of all the people that don't believe in gimmicks, that's me. But at the time it sounded good. I was looking for a dollar the quick way and I was trying to get my foot in the door and become a personality. It lasted for about a year and after that I gave it up and went right back to straight wrestling."

Sabre by pro wrestling standards wasn't very big. He was about five foot ten and weighed one hundred and eighty five pounds. At the time we did our story on the wrestling school, Bob was fifty one years old and as they say, had been around the block a few times. Sabre had some strong views on the mat game, feeling that promoters had gone over board with too much emphasis on showboating:

"I would like to change everything and go back to the clean stuff. But I don't know if the public would buy it. We need a change in wrestling. I think showmanship has gone too far. All we've got now are big gorillas and wrestlers with bleached blonde hair."

Although Sabre was campaigning for clean, scientific wrestling, he realized that straight matches, strictly on the up and up would not draw. And he conceded that you've got to give the fans what they want.

Bob Sabre never lived long enough to see if some of his young charges make it big time in the ring. Although he kept in tip top condition he was stricken with cancer and died a short time later.

Meanwhile, the beat goes on. New villains and new "baby faces" as the good guys are called have come to the fore. The taste in villains has changed too. Nazis and Cossacks are out, Arabs and biker types are in.

But one thing remains constant. Pro wrestling fans like their matmen big. Heroes and villains have one thing in common. They are usually behemoths. As the saying goes, "The bigger they are, the harder they fall."

THE SANDMAN

Johnny Revolta didn't belt 'em long off the tees but the Wisconsin native made up for his shortcomings with a driver by honing a super short game. Revolta was an excellent putter and when it came to getting out of a sand trap, Johnny was in a league by himself.

For years Revolta was the head pro at the Evanston Golf Club which is located just outside of Chicago. The curly haired Revolta was best known as a teacher. He not only gave lessons to hackers and duffers but helped sharpen the game of touring professionals including some of the biggest names on the women's golf circuit.

Before Revolta began spending a lot of time on the lessons tee, he followed the sun, competing on what was then the fledgling PGA circuit. When Johnny entered the play for pay ranks in 1933 the tour was a far cry from what it is today. There were fewer tournaments and the purses were minuscule compared to the cash bonanzas handed out each Sunday in the television era. Revolta claimed to have won nineteen PGA sanctioned tournaments including two major championships. Not bad for a kid who got his start at a municipal course in Oshkosh, Wisconsin.

John Daley and Tiger Woods weren't around when Johnny made his pro debut in the early 30s. But even then the game had it's share of long hitters. Fellows like Jimmy Thomson, Johnny Bulla, and Sam Snead could hold their own even with the big hitters of the 1990s

Despite being outdriven by the vast majority of his opponents Revolta didn't become discouraged. He made the most of what he had, a brilliant short game. It paid off! In 1935 Revolta won five tournaments. Very few of today's touring pros can boast of such an accomplishment.

One of those victories came at the PGA championship which was a match play affair in that era. Revolta was only twenty four years old when he upset the legendary Walter Hagen, a five time PGA champion in the opening round. Hagen was heavily favored to beat Revolta. But the underdog stunned the "Haig" as Revolta made seven outstanding recovery shots from sand traps for either pars or birdies. Revolta won the match on the final hole, one up.

Revolta's short game continued to sizzle as he advanced to the finals where he was again in the underdog role. His opponent in the championship match was Tommy Armour, one of the greatest iron players of all time. Revolta, though had little trouble with the Scotchman, winning the 36 hole match 5 and 4. Again it was Johnny's short game which proved the difference. Revolta one putted thirteen greens en route to victory.

Revolta also won the Western Open in 1935 which was held that year at the South Bend Country Club. In the period before World War II, the Western was considered a major championship.

In an interview with this writer, years after Revolta had quit playing competitive golf, Johnny told me that his ability to get out of a bunker didn't come naturally. Revolta said his skill in blasting out of the sand was the result of practice making perfect. The veteran professional explained his secret this way: "As a kid I got a job at the Oshkosh municipal course. When my boss went home to lunch, I'd spend an hour in the sand traps. I think that's when I really got my start. I could do anything out of a sand trap. Burn it, close it, burn it high, burn it low. Getting out of a trap is all touch and feel."

Revolta, with five victories in 1935, was the leading money winner on the tour that year. His prize money amounted to ninety five hundred dollars, a pauper's sum compared to what the hot shots earn in the modern era.

In Revolta's day, professionals got their education in the college of hard knocks. Future pros earned their stripes starting as caddies, then moving up to become caddymasters, eventually getting an assistant pro job. Then if they had the right contacts, aspiring pros might land a coveted position as a head professional at a country club. In the 1930s and 40s the head pro had to be a Jack of all trades. Not only did he sell merchandise in the pro shop and give lessons but the pro was expected to be competent in repairing golf clubs. He often had to bow to the whims of various club members, some of whom could be hard to get along with.

But that was where the money was and a good club job was hard to find in those depression years. The purses were too small to make a living by just playing in tournaments. There were a few exceptions of course, but by and large even the big name pros, the Nelsons, the Hogans, and the Sneads, all had jobs at country clubs. In 1936 Revolta caught on as head professional at the Evanston club. It meant a steady pay check and decent working conditions. The arrangement must have been mutually agreeable since Revolta literally became an icon at the north shore course.

Not all golf pros had such an easy transition from the circuit to a country club. Back then golf pros were seen in some circles as uncouth riff raff. They were not supposed to mingle socially with the blue bloods that filled the membership ranks. That's all changed now. But there was a time when pros were looked down upon. A pro had to know his place. That was usually defined as the pro shop or the lesson tee.

Revolta and the Evanston golf club had a love affair that lasted more than thirty years. Actually Revolta never completely severed his connection to Evanston. In Johnny's later years, when he spent most of his time at the Mission Hills Country Club at Rancho Mirage, California, Revolta was the pro emeritus at the Evanston club. Unlike many other private clubs there is little turnover at Evanston. Hal Miller who succeeded Revolta remains, as of this writing, as the head pro at the club.

In his role as pro emeritus at Evanston Revolta would return each summer where he could often be found working his magic in a sand trap. Revolta's skills may have diminished but he never lost his touch around the greens. When Revolta lobbed wedge shots out of a trap there were usually a number of members on hand trying to learn the master's secrets.

Johnny Revolta, "The Sandman." Had an outstanding short game that enabled him to beat his longer-hitting opponents.

Revolta's reputation as a teacher soon spread well beyond the Chicago area. He collaborated on a book with Chicago newspaperman Charles Cleveland. The book enabled Revolta to pass on his secrets as a sand saver to the golfing public.

Revolta in his later years worked a lot with youngsters, becoming one of the bigger boosters of junior golf in the midwest. We observed Revolta giving a lesson to a youngster one day. Revolta, with a drink in one hand and a wedge in the other, was laid back, speaking calmly to a pre-teen who was trying, without any luck, to get out of a sand trap. Revolta then anchored his feet in the sand and blasted out of the "beach" sending the golf ball within inches of the pin. Revolta must have inspired the youngster because before long the pupil was following suit.

Johnny in some ways emulated his former tour rival, Tommy Armour when it came to giving lessons. Revolta could usually tell where a student's sand shot was going without following the ball. That was "SOP" with the silvery haired Armour. Revolta reminisced one time with me about Armour's techniques: "He (Armour) would sit under an umbrella. He wouldn't even follow the flight of

237

the ball. He (Armour) would have a caddy say which way the ball would go and the caddy would say left or right. And Armour would tell the pupil what to do."

Tommy Armour was a golf guru but Revolta didn't fare too badly in that capacity either. Remember, when Revolta started giving lessons golfers were using wooden shafted clubs. A two wood was called a brassie, a three wood was labeled a spoon, and a two iron was known as a mid-iron. Despite the technological advances in the game, graphite shafts, metal headed drivers, grooved irons, and balata balls, Revolta's sand savers are as up to date now as they were sixty years ago. A club can do so much. The golfer still has to make the shot. And that's why you need and will always need a skilled professional to tell you how to do it.

Although no bunker was ever built that could hold Johnny Revolta father time did. Heart and circulation problems took their toll. In March of 1991 Johnny Revolta died in Palm Springs. He was seventy nine.

But Revolta will always remain an inspiration to golfers whose drives leaves something to be desired. Revolta proved that a short hitter can be competitive if he or she can work some magic around the greens. That's something Revolta was always able to do.

MR. QUARTERBACK

Chicagoans will put up with a lot of things without squawking too much. They are able to grin and bear it when a snowstorm slams into the city. Commuters accept gridlock on the expressways as par for the course. And when a favorite Alderman gets caught with his "fingers in the cookie jar," most residents don't bother to even raise an eyebrow.

But when the Bears lose a football game, especially to the arch-rival Green Bay Packers, that's another story. Those defeats are treated in the same vein as famine, pestilence, and bubonic plague. In other words a Bears loss is considered a disaster in some circles. If you think I'm pulling your leg, listen to a radio talk show after a Bears loss and you'll get the message.

Chicagoans get uptight when their beloved "Monsters of the Midway" take it on the chin. The fans want to take out their wrath on someone, the owner, the coach, the QB, the halfbacks, the guys in the trenches, even the media. They are all targets of the boo birds. I know from first hand experience, having done a number of live shots outside of Soldier Field immediately following a game in which the Bears lost. Some disgruntled fans who have had more than their share of "firewater" are ready to go off the deep end. In several instances we had to terminate our report and throw it back to the studio before mayhem erupted.

The reader may say, pro football fans are the same all over the country. Chicago doesn't have a monopoly on sore losers. That's true up to a point. In every NFL market there are hard-core fans who can't take it when their favorites go down the tubes. But by and large most fans in those communities don't get that uptight when their heroes fail to measure up. Take Packer fans. Even in the team's bad years, when losses far outnumbered victories, most Packer fans didn't rip their team or management. You see, the logic in the northland went something like this, true Packer fans didn't bum rap the team or the coach.

No folks, Bears fans won't tolerate mediocrity. In my view the fans were spoiled by early successes when the franchise dominated the NFL. With the exception of the Packers the Bears have won more championships than any other pro football team. At one time the Bears were the New York Yankees of football. That was certainly the case in the 1940s when the Bears, except for two wartime seasons, posted a phenomenal record. That was the golden era for Chicago. The team won NFL titles in 1940, 41, 43, and 46. In 1942 the team was unbeaten in regular season play but lost to the Redskins in the title game. The Bears also had excellent teams in 47, 48, 49, and 50. That was the decade when the Bears drubbed Washington 73 to 0 in the most lopsided championship game in history.

Those Bears teams were loaded with players of all star caliber. And one who stood out in a galaxy of stars was a former Ivy Leaguer who was dubbed "Mr. Quarterback" by coach George Halas. That was former Columbia star Sid Luckman, an NFL Hall-of-Famer.

Long after he retired we did several lengthy interviews with Luckman at his posh Lake Shore Drive condominium. And on one occasion I let Sid reminisce about those glory years with the Bears.

Luckman, a native of Brooklyn, went to Columbia after a fabled prep career at Erasmus High School. Columbia, under the legendary Lou Little, didn't have many good teams. But Luckman stood out as a pass throwing single wing tailback for the Lions. Luckman told me he had no intention of turning pro after his collegiate career was over. He planned to go into the trucking business with his brothers. However, Luckman didn't realize how persuasive owner-coach Halas could be.

Halas had watched Luckman and his Columbia gridders play Army at Baker Field. And Halas came away impressed with the talents of the young Ivy Leaguer. The canny Halas was already envisioning Luckman as the quarterback in a new-fangled formation he was planning to unleash. It was the T formation with a man in motion. It would revolutionize football on both the professional and collegiate level. But Luckman at first was hesitant to take the plunge: "I really didn't want to play professional football, never realizing I was ever going to be good enough, coming out of the Ivy League."

Luckman had a change of heart when Halas offered him a then unheard of salary for a rookie of five thousand dollars Luckman was hooked. Although Luckman admits money was a factor in his decision to join the play for pay ranks, it was Halas' assurances that he wanted to coach only winners that put frosting on the cake: "He (Halas) told me he would do anything in his power to see that the team was dominant, that the team was going to be victorious, and he thought I could play a part in it."

And play a part he did. Luckman was with the Bears for twelve seasons, setting a number of passing records for the team that still haven't been bettered.

Don't get the idea that the Bears were a one man show in that era. Luckman had a strong supporting cast including backs like George Mcafee, Hugh Gallarneau, and Bill Osmanski. Then there were hall of fame lineman such as "Bulldog' Turner, Joe Stydahar, Dr. Danny Fortmann, and George Musso. By pre-war standards the Bears were a big team able to overpower their opponents. Luckman always stressed that point: "It wasn't a small team even by the standards of today. Our line averaged two hundred and forty five pounds which was a very dominant factor. The fact was, we could overpower most of the teams we played."

But size wasn't the only thing that was a factor in garnering those championship trophies. Luckman said the Bears had almost a fanatical desire to win: "We were totally dedicated to victory. We were so intent on winning, winning was almost everything for us. And when we did lose a game, and we did lose a few, you could feel the emotional letdown. The boys were actually crying in the dressing room."

The Bears' greatest quarterback. Photo courtesy The Chicago Bears.

There was no question that the Bears were ahead of their time in the early 1940s. While other clubs used the single wing, Halas' T-formation with a man in motion gave defenders fits. As Luckman explained: "They (the opposition) did not really know how to play against the T-formation. They didn't know how to defense it."

Soon everybody got into the act. On the college scene, Stanford switched to the T in 1940. The Indians, as they were called back then, were unbeaten and went on to defeat Nebraska in the Rose

Bowl. While on the pro front it wasn't long before every team converted to the T. The Pittsburgh Steelers were the lone holdout. But they too finally saw the light. Luckman felt the "father" of the modern day T was too shy to take credit when credit was due: "I always told coach Halas, it should have been called the Halas formation. But he resisted that. Knowing how humble he was and the kind of man he was, he insisted upon using the name T-formation and that's where it stands today."

Age finally caught up with the Bears organization. By 1950 the nucleus of the team that had been so dominant was aging. Some had retired and others who continued to put on the pads were over the hill. Luckman although still effective at thirty four decided to call it quits after the 1950 campaign. By then he had rewritten the Bears record book. He tossed 137 td passes in his career including seven in just one game. He had over 14-thousand yards passing at a time when the running game was King of the hill.

Although Luckman became a successful Chicago businessman with no apparent financial worries he remained a Bear for years, serving as an unpaid assistant to coach Halas. Luckman was on the sidelines in 1963, as a coach, when Halas won his last NFL crown.

Luckman's tenure with the Bears left an indelible mark on him. Sitting in his living room, almost forty years after his playing days, Luckman, his voice choking with emotion, told me: "They were marvelous, marvelous years. When I look back at those years, you can take away everything from me as a human being, but you can never take away the glorious moments of being a member of the legendary and fabulous Chicago Bears."

EPILOGUE

From a technological standpoint the business has changed considerably since I entered the broadcast journalism field in the 1950s. Watergate brought a flood of eager young newspeople into the fifth estate in the early 1970s. That was a time when video tape, mini cams, and live shots were coming to the fore. The 1980s and 90s brought more technological advancements, including satellite feeds, which revolutionized the broadcast landscape.

Baghdad and other heretofore remote locations became as accessible as the nearest suburb. Local TV reporters began cropping up doing live shots from war zones and foreign capitals just as their colleagues had been doing at City Hall and the School Board. The technology only intensified the fierce competition between TV stations in trying to get a "leg up" on the other guy.

Many TV stations retain outside news consultants, known as "news doctors." They often dictate or at least strongly recommend the type of coverage contained in a daily newscast. The result is, many newscasts appear the same in story content whether the outlet is in Tulsa, Oklahoma or Cleveland, Ohio. Thus, the breaking of a big story or an exclusive interview, particularly in a sweeps period, gives the station an identity which can provide a huge ratings boost.

A case in point. WBBM-TV in Chicago did an exclusive interview with mass murderer John Wayne Gacy. The ratings went through the roof when the series on Gacy aired. Unfortunately from the station's point of view, the ratings flattened out drastically after the Gacy series was wrapped up. Sometimes, though, a big exclusive can have a lasting effect in propelling the newscast to the top of the heap or at least to parity with rival news operations.

Because there is gold in those hills with an exclusive, news directors are constantly urging their troops to hit paydirt. That can lead to rushes in judgment by reporters and producers, to put an exclusive on the air before solid sources are contacted for some semblance of verification.

I'll give you an example of that. It happened in a large eastern city where station X was trying to bolster it's ratings on the five o'clock news. The station carried a story linking the mayor of that city with a kickback scheme. Station X went on the air hyping the story that said in effect that the city's chief executive was a crook.

Station X had to eat crow. The mayor was not convicted of any wrongdoing. There was no solid evidence that the mayor was corrupt. A nasty lawsuit followed, eventually leading to changes in the station's hierarchy.

The then U.S. Attorney for that large city later told me that station X had never called him to ask if the allegations about the mayor were true. The station had alluded to a Federal probe. If Federal authorities were checking out the mayor, such an investigation would have been handled by the U.S. Attorney's office. A phone call to the U.S. Attorney might have saved the station a big chunk of cash and a lot of embarrassment.

Most often an official will say no comment when questioned about an ongoing investigation. But there are some ways to circumvent such nondescript responses. Sometimes rephrasing a question about an ongoing probe can be productive. I recall on more than one occasion asking a source if it was likely the station would be sued successfully if we ran with the story. Another question to the official might go like this: If we aired the material, would the subject of the story have any real grounds for filing legal action? If the source replied no to either question, I felt I was on the right track.

On the other hand, there are some sources who are so concerned about making any kind of comment that they become so defensive that it's almost ludicrous. I remember one guy who was so worried about leaks that if you had asked him the time of day he probably would have clammed up. Frankly if you had asked this man if the sun was shining he would have prefaced his remarks by saying "According to the U.S. Weather Bureau the skies are clear and there is plenty of sunshine." Obviously this guy played it as close to the vest as anybody I ever had contact with.

Self imposed deadlines by news brass to get an exclusive on the air by such and such a date can result in sloppy reporting and editing. An investigative report by a network owned Chicago station about the pending indictment of a local Teamster official proved to be an embarrassment.

The case against the Teamster official had basically collapsed by the time the report was aired. We knew about the case and were intending, at one time, to do a piece about it. But we lost interest after we were told that the Justice Department in Washington had vetoed the recommendation by prosecutors in the U.S. Attorneys office in Chicago to seek an indictment against the man. Reportedly the Washington "honchos" felt that the allegations against the Teamsters official were not strong enough to proceed with any legal action.

The other station went on the air trumpeting the story as an exclusive. But in the rush to get the piece edited someone, a producer or reporter, made a serious error. In showing video of the subject, who they alleged was the target of the investigation, they identified the wrong man.

They took a clip from a Columbus day parade in Chicago highlighting a man on the reviewing stand as the Teamster official who was about to be indicted. The man the station identified as the Teamster official was none other than a Congressman, Frank Annunzio. Annunzio was not the subject of any Teamsters investigation. To say that the miscue put a damper on the exclusive would be the understatement of the year.

A pending indictment always fits into the food chain of exclusives. But reporters have to be sure they've got the goods before publicly airing their information. Even if the reporter is right on the beam an overly cautious news director can derail that exclusive. One time at Channel Two in Chicago we had reliable information that a Federal grand jury would be returning an indictment the next day against a prominent judge. We knew the information was "gospel" because the judges' lawyer confirmed to us that the Justice Department had called him (the attorney) and told him so.

I went into the news director's office to propose that we run with the story. To my surprise the news director didn't buy the idea. He asked me if I could guarantee that the indictment would be returned the next day. Of course I couldn't give a one hundred percent guarantee. After all the jury foreman could be stricken during the night and the indictment would be held up a for a day or two. I also couldn't guarantee that an earthquake wouldn't rock the Chicago area in the next twenty four hours also putting the indictment on hold. Then I pointed out that you could write around any such possible disasters by telling our viewers that Channel Two news had learned that prosecutors will seek an indictment against the judge. That way, if by some odd twist of fate, the indictment was not returned the next day we had covered ourselves. But the news director wasn't impressed and our exclusive went down the drain. Oh yes, the judge was indicted the next day as we expected. It was the lead story on all the local newscasts.

Government officials have a tendency to go "bananas" when they feel they have a leak in their organization. Despite such suspicions, there is often no leak at all. A reporter sometimes can put two and two together. For example, a reporter sees a lawyer with his client in the lobby or hallway of a courthouse. The lawyer is known as an expert when it comes to plea bargaining. Deduction, lawyer is coming to see prosecutors about making a deal for his client. Deduction, client will probably plead guilty and very possibly end up cooperating with the government. Deduction, if he cooperates, it could lead to more indictments.

Sometimes a camera crew happens to be at the right place at the right time. On one occasion, all of the major news outlets in Chicago were alerted that the U.S. Attorneys Office would be holding a news conference the following day to announce the arrest of a number of major drug dealers. Nobody ran the story that night. Doing so would have jeopardized the arrests and raids that were scheduled to take place the following morning. Although the authorities had tipped us off about the news conference they would not reveal the locations of the raids.

We held a strategy session that night in an effort to determine where the action would be in the A.M. We were hoping to get shots of agents making the actual arrests so we could get a jump over the competition. The competition, meanwhile, was doing the same thing we were, trying to pinpoint the site of the raids.

We received no inside information from any of the government people involved in the story. We had a lot of potential real estate to consider before sending our troops out to capture the action on videotape. Remember the Chicago metropolitan area is a big chunk of terra firma which includes northwest Indiana. We did not have the luxury in time or manpower to send out mini cam crews on a longshot that they might come just stumble across something.

We decided to concentrate our troops in a neighborhood in Chicago where the notorious Herrera drug smuggling family operated. As luck would have it, one crew was parked near a gas station in that neck of the woods when a convoy of FBI agents, the tires on their cars squealing, pulled into the service station. It was a great way to open our coverage that night. The squealing tires, the agents jumping from their cars and invading the headquarters of one of the alleged drug Kingpins.

One of the other TV stations got word of our gas station coup and complained to the U.S. Attorney in Chicago. They charged that a Channel Two news crew was either riding with the agents or had been tipped off as to the whereabouts of the raids. The then U.S. Attorney, Anton Valukas, called me on the phone, saying if the rival stations' allegations were true, the person leaking the information to us would face dismissal or even criminal charges. We assured Mr. Valukas that no government agent was riding in our vehicles and that no one had tipped us to be at a certain location. It was just a case of being in the right place at the right time.

In some cases another kind of vehicle is needed to provide the news department with the video they need to spice up a story. TV news directors soon realized, as the allies and axis powers did during World War II, that air superiority could turn the tide. Most TV stations in major markets either own or lease their own helicopters. For shots of floods, natural disasters, fire or crime scenes the chopper is hard to beat. It's routine to see choppers covering rush hour traffic or chase scenes on the expressways (remember O.J.). An enterprising news or assignment editor can judiciously use his own "Luftwaffe" to get shots that are normally inaccessible.

We once did a profile on Joe Ferriola, then a rising star with the Chicago Mob. Ferriola had a gorgeous home in the western suburbs and a fancy looking retreat at Green Lake, Wisconsin where he entertained his underlings in grand style. We needed to show our viewers that, like other CEO's, Ferriola, had a lifestyle befitting his status with the Chicago Outfit. We had no difficulty in getting pictures of his home in Oak Brook but the property in Wisconsin was another matter. The Green Lake home was secluded and there was no way we could get video from the road. We opted to order an air strike. Our "Luftwaffe," in this case was a helicopter which was brought into play. The chopper did it's job, making several low passes over the Ferriola property. The video revealed not only a fancy looking cottage but a big boathouse and dock as well. It was frosting on the cake. The shots from the helicopter beefed up the piece. The air strike was worth the cost involved in sending the helicopter up to central Wisconsin.

Nowadays news departments even in smaller markets have larger staffs. A generation ago "talent" whether they were newspersons or staff announcers had to wear a number of hats. I found that out in my first television job in Rockford, Illinois.

In the spring of 1960, after several years as a radio newsman, I began sending out resumes to television stations in the upper midwest. I received replies from only a couple of station managers, but one of them, WREX-TV in Rockford, Illinois, invited me to audition for an undisclosed position at the station. The opening, I found out, was for a combination news and sports post at Channel 13.

After writing and reading a short newscast I was instructed to do the same for a sportscast. Apparently the station executives liked or at least weren't turned off by my efforts. At any rate I was summoned to an office where management explained to me that the station was looking for someone who would work as a news reporter during the day and then write and air a ten minute sportscast six nights a week.

The sportscast was sponsored three nights a week by the Joseph Schlitz brewing company. There would be two commercials on each show, one on film the other would be live. I was a Schlitz drinker at the time so that didn't appear to be a problem for me, even though I had never done a live television commercial before or for that matter any kind of TV commercial.

But there was one potential fly in the ointment. The Schlitz distributor in Rockford who was footing a good chunk of the dough for the sportscast was insistent on one point. He was concerned that when the talent poured the Schlitz into a pilsener glass that the beer would have no head and thus appear flat. That he explained, would be counter productive and would turn beer drinkers away from Schlitz to another brand. Remember this was before videotape. The commercial was live and there could only be one take. I could have the job, I was told, with the proviso that I came through with flying colors on the "beer exam."

That was my introduction to television. I get a job as a sports director/newsman if I make a decent showing doing a beer commercial. So what few guns I had in my arsenal I had to use. It was time for a few tricks of the trade. I poured a little salt into the pilsener glass where it settled on the bottom. Now I was ready for the acid test.

Be advised, I was facing the camera reading from a primitive teleprompter and could only glance at the glass as I poured the Schlitz into it. At the same time I was extolling the virtues of the "Beer that Made Milwaukee Famous." Call it luck, call it divine intervention, there was a perfect head on the beer and the job was mine.

Fortunately the program department soon came to the conclusion that it was asking too much for the talent to do the actual pouring, while he was doing a sportscast. So a stage hand was given the unenviable task of pouring beer into the pilsener glass while I read the commercial. I was home free.

The coveted position I obtained through the bone chilling audition paid a princely sum of one hundred dollars a week. That was for a six day work week with a seventh day occasionally thrown in when conditions warranted. When I came on board I didn't know that in addition to news and sports duties, I also had to "tape the book" two nights a week. That meant I would go into the announce booth after the ten o'clock show and read all the breaks and public service announcements until sign off. I was also required to record all of the breaks from sign on the next day until the time the booth announcer was scheduled to come on duty in the early afternoon. It made for some long days but that was what small market television was all about in the early 60s. My case was no different than most aspiring newsmen or sportscasters who were toiling in small market trenches in that era.

Management had you over a barrel. If you didn't like the six day work week and marathon hours, no problem. They could find someone else who would be willing to work for peanuts just for a chance to make it in television.

Although the technical aspects of the business continue to move, it seems with the speed of light, some things never change. After auditioning successfully for the Rockford job I was ushered into the offices of the station's general manager, Joe Baisch. Channel 13's sales manager Al Bilardello began a hard sell outlining Drummond's credentials. Drummond, Al said "Was a former Air Force instructor who had a master's degree and solid work experience, including a stint at a fifty thousand watt radio station." Al poured it on, telling Baisch that I had also done play by play as well as having conducted a radio sports show.

Baisch listened intently and then turned to both of us and said "That's all well and good. But can he get me any numbers?"

Ratings were the name of the game in 1960 and it hasn't changed one iota. Videotape, mini cams, and satellite feeds are great tools in helping present information to the general public. But for the anchorman and anchorwoman who front the newscasts and the news director and often the station general manager who are responsible for the talent and the overall operation of the newsroom it's "no tickee, no laundry." In other words, get the numbers or get out. It's the nature of the beast. If you can't adjust to that you shouldn't be in the business.